DISCARD STUDIES IN INDIA

A Case of Patna

DISCARD STUDIES IN INDIA

A Case of Patna

Papia Raj and Aditya Raj

Published by

Kalpaz Publications
C-30, Satyawati Nagar,
Delhi – 110052
Ph.: 011-47034999, 9811692060
www.kalpazpublications.com
E-mail: kalpaz@hotmail.com

Distribution Network
gyanbooks.com
India, USA, Canada, UK, Australia, France

ISBN: 978-93-5722-277-8 (HB)

First Published, 2023

Printed at: Gyan Press, Delhi.

DISCARD STUDIES IN INDIA: A CASE OF PATNA
Authors: PAPIA RAJ AND ADITYA RAJ

Preface

We moved to Patna as a family in the summer of 2010 when one of us joined the Indian Institute of Technology Patna (IITP), Bihar and the other joined the Central University of Bihar (now, Central University of South Bihar). These institutions were in their nascent phase and the crescendo of hope was rising for a better Bihar. After our M.A. (Master of Arts) and M.Phil. (Master of Philosophy), both of us had received Commonwealth Scholarship for our doctoral research at Canada's McGill University. India's Ministry of Human Resource Development had selected us and first recommended us for the scholarship. Soon after completing our doctorate and post-doctorate in Canada, returning to Bihar's capital Patna was exciting for us. As we settled in and traversed the academic, social, cultural, health, and political spaces in Patna, we became aware of the importance about status of people and practices along with discard of some products by human practices. We were intrigued by what the space offered for studies. Just then came the pronouncement of the High Court of Judicature at Patna in 2010, which while chiding the Patna Municipal Corporation (PMC) called Patna the garbage city of India.

We were perplexed and followed with review of published work, historical records, and several rounds of discussions to rigorously comprehend the situation in this historical city. Dr Papia explored the health implications more while Dr Aditya located the lack of public education. Dr Papia joined IIT Patna in 2013. Together we submitted a research proposal to the Centre for Energy and Environment- one of the Centres of Excellence, then, at

IITP, under the stewardship of honourable Director Professor Anil Bhowmick. We got research collaborators from other departments at IITP. A financial grant helped us carry out detailed research.

Support was received from several quarters. Professor Ashok Ghosh stood by us in academic discussions, in our workshops, and over phone. He is now the Chairman of Bihar State Pollution Control Board, and Member, Regional Empowered Committee of Ministry of Environment, Forest, and Climate Change Government of India. We would like to mention Dr Bindeshwar Pathak, the founder of Sulabh International Social Service Organisation. While Professor Ashok Ghosh was the chief guest in our first project workshop, Dr Bindeshwar Pathak graced the second one wherein more than fifty schools of Patna district were involved. Delhi Public School Patna, principal and teachers were active participants. Sr SudhaVerghese joined the discussion in the evening for the valedictory.

Field information collection would not have been possible without the support of our research assistants and interns. Our PhD students like Manish, Pooja, and Vibhuti also chipped in during workshops. We also supported another student with financial assistance and our fieldwork data. Dr Pathak at MahabirVatsalaya Hospital, Kuldip Narayan at PMC, Kaushlendra from *Kaushilya* Foundation, Praveen More at UNICEF Patna, and Ratnish at *Nidan* deserve special mention for being there during the initial phase of the research that forms the kernel of this book. We shared our research with various forums of repute. From this research, we together published in the *International Sociological Association e- Symposium* and in *Mainstream*. We wrote a book chapter in Professor Manish Verma edited book *Globalisation, Environment, and Social Justice: Perspectives, Issues, and Concerns.* Dr Papia was the PI (principal investigator) of our project and she published in other academic venues also.

We organised a GIAN (Global Initiative of Academic Networks) course on Waste Management and Health Care. The foreign expert was Dr Pankaj Lal from the Department of Earth and Environmental Studies and founding director of Clean Energy and Sustainability

Analytics, Montclair State University. There were participants from several academic institutions. We have tried to involve national and international experts. In the book, we have covered discussion on China, India, Nepal for instance. We have compared Patna with Delhi as well. All these are done to compare and provide holistic understanding. The last chapter of the book significantly covers issues from Covid and post-Covid period.

We would like to dedicate this effort to our teachers who taught us to include everyone and treat all products of Mother Nature with respect. We hope for a better comprehension of what is discard- not just product but also practices that guides social relations of people with people and people with products. We are interested in waste to energy. Some aspects are covered and hopefully some more will be dealt with in due course of time. We are sure that together we can make our planet a better place to live- loveable and sustainable.

Papia Raj and Aditya Raj

Contents

List of Tables and Figures

Tables

Figures

1

Introduction

Discard studies can be understood as a field of study that tries to highlight people and practices considered outside the main gaze of life and times. It is an attempt to include excluded people, practices, and products as well as construct knowledge about them for the benefit of all. Although we have been studying several excluded social issues but the concern here is with those considered menial product- waste. It is not just waste that need to be seen (as waste can be easily seen) but the socio-cultural, economic, and political attitude that creates the so-called obvious waste products.

Discard studies can be considered as an interdisciplinary attempt to contextualise a social problem, look at it comprehensively from more than one standpoint, and hope for approaches that will be useful for our people and our planet. Very simple, and obvious, example are the authors themselves. One author is a geographer with specialisation in public health whose prime devotion is preventive health of people especially in so-called under-developed regions of the world. The other author has a multi-disciplinary background in history, journalism, sociology, and his central desire is public education. Together, they situate one of their research on waste production and management in one city of India.

Besides, urge for social inclusion and inter-disciplinary, discard studies can also be perceived from intersectional perspectives because we need to understand social production of waste in its historical, politico-economic, and social context. The rubric of discard studies may be new to India but, we reiterate, work around it have been done. We intend to set a step to funnel the voluminous work and use a bit to situate our research on issues of waste production and waste management. Discard studies will be very useful to comprehend Indian society further.

We think "study" as the site of pedagogy conveys learning and understanding; competence augmentation, self reflection, and self actualisation; inquiry, experiment and "re-search;" as well as spaces such as school, library, community, and their like. Therefore, the choice of "studies" in the title is to foster passion of learning and understanding, develop clarity of thought and expression with individual or team researchers on the subject matter, and value research participant's partnership in knowledge production and dissemination. When we study, we energetically try to draw ourselves to not only the content of what is under study but also the context in which and from which it is drawn. Therefore, study makes us consider what is being studied as well as how its meaning configures in its history as well as in its emergent context.

Discard studies in India will be a valuable addition because we have been studying caste system, caste mobility, and its various dimensions and in all we identify the interplay of the concept of pollution and purity. The labyrinth of what is pure and what is deliberated polluted is helpful to proliferate the grounding of discard studies in India. What is considered polluted (product) or polluting (practices) are what concerns us for this work. Caste system is pivotal since the polluted caste were historically referred as very polluted- untouchable. The work that untouchables did were the realm of what was discarded by the so-called not polluted (or, pure). This practice of untouchability had grounding in what is considered not required or to be discarded. Mahatma Gandhi's effort to stop manual scavenging should remind us of the deep seated issue of how discarded people did throwing away of the discard to further discarded spaces. As students of education and public health, we have deeply reflected on the knowledge creation and its social of what might have started and sustained such inhuman practice-untouchability.

Today, things have changed a fair bit. However, we need to go miles. We need to make sure that other forms of occlusion does not perpetuate. Occlusion is a practice where there is obstruction to rational contextual forms of knowledge. Under the garb of development, there are processes and discourses to erase local practices. This is important when we know that indigenous communities knew how to live life in consonance with Mother Nature. Rampant capitalism and conspicuous consumption creates more waste. Moreover, factory production and mass consumption does not teach how to take care of waste produced. While the developed corporate countries have learnt to hide their waste sooner, the developing and under-developed countries are learning to hide their waste in landfills. We repeat- hide the waste. Recycle and reuse is thrown in the mix of things for the sake of sustainability.

We moor our research in Patna on waste production and waste management in discard studies. Patna is the capital city of Bihar. This province is known for its rich history. In fact, and as pronounced by a famous Indian historian, the history of ancient India is the history of Bihar. Nevertheless, the current situation is alarming so much so that the High Court of Judicature at Patna in 2010 while chiding the Patna Municipal Corporation (PMC) pronounced Patna as the garbage city of India. Therefore, Patna is unique and most appropriate as a case in the study of discard studies in India. There are efforts, these days by PMC, which is interesting as well. We will get to examining the specificities soon after setting the broader contours of the study.

Sociological perspective on waste

Human population is rising exponentially and activities to either fulfil basic life necessities or improve lifestyle of masses result in the production of more waste materials. Consequently, the ever-increasing quantities of waste have attracted the attention of governments, scholars, and activists, and the issue of waste has risen up rapidly at the global level. Along with these developments, research into waste has surged both in anthropology and across the social sciences and humanities, giving rise to the interdisciplinary subfield of discard studies.With the recent emergence across the social sciences, waste has often been portrayed as residue from production or consumption processes, although there might be different opinions of how this is to be classified. Mary Douglas, in her seminal work *Purity and Danger* (1992) conceptualised the famous notion of dirt as 'matter out of place', from which scholars concluded that dirt, waste, and trash are dynamic categories (Drackner, 2005). This concept by Douglas assumes 'waste' to be something unwanted or discarded, as well as the opposite and symbolic counterpart of a valued treasure. Hence, dirt, or waste for that matter is relational by definition which implies that one man's waste may be another man's livelihood or as Strasser (1999) argues what counts as trash depends on who's counting.

According to the *Cambridge Encyclopedia of Anthropology* (2020), there are three analytic approaches to waste taken by anthropologists, presented and explained by Alexander and O'Hare (2019): symbolic-structuralist; economic-materialist; and posthuman-intersubjective. In symbolic-structuralist approach (Douglas, 1966; Leach, 1989), waste can be understood as what emerges through interactions between the sacred and profane, which are structurally bound to one another. In this perspective, waste is considered to be social and relational rather than an objective quality or categorisation of phenomena in the world. In *Purity and Danger* (1968), Douglas believes that prohibitions, taboos, and attachments have very little to do with the concrete thing that is prohibited, and much more to do with an interplay of symbols that considers deeper organising principles of society. For her, cultural classification comes first and determines ideas of pollution. However, scholars such as O'Brien (2008) criticised her ideas in part because phrasing dirt or waste, so concisely as 'matter out of place' defamiliarises one from the notion that what constitutes waste should be apparent and universally accepted. Also, since Douglas was more interested in the symbolism of ritual pollution in religion, she was considered unsuitable for discussions of the billions of tons of solid waste that arrive daily at the landfills (O'Brien, 2008).

The second analytical approach, indicated by Michael Thompson's (1979) *Rubbish Theory*, set forth an economic-materialist approach to understand the circulation of materials between different regimes of value. His theory brought in another important binary: waste and value. Thompson uses a tripartite concept to help understand how objects can undergo radical transformations in value. He begins with two categories of goods common to economics: transient and durable. An important example of a transient good is a car, which decreases in value from the time that it is bought until it is reduced to scrap, while durables, such as certain antiques, increase in value over time and have infinite life-spans (O'Hare, 2019). Thompson's primary fascination lies in how an object can transform from one category to the other, as they do in the case of old cars, or antiques. The question brings on a new third category for goods that are neither decreasing nor increasing in value but are of no value at all: rubbish. He describes the rubbish stage as denoting a value-less state, which later moves into the category of durables – never seems to attain the state of zero value. Thompson's rubbish category is thus restricted to a class of objects that still have owners, have decreased in value, but have not been disposed of.

A third approach to the study of waste is 'posthuman-intersubjective'. This notion is gaining strength since the 2010s and focuses on the subjects that waste and various forms of waste-work engender. This includes workers whose identities are closely associated with waste – such as waste-pickers (Millar, 2018), as well as the most common encounters with discarded materials that happen as we separate our recyclables (Hawkins, 2006), or accidentally meet with a heap of waste in the street (Bennett, 2009). In this perspective, waste is given different degrees of agency: it is seen as acting and acting upon us in ways that are outside our conscious control. Creating subjectivities by engaging with waste is similar to actor-network theory (ANT) where waste itself has agency (Hawkins, 2006).

Social recognition of waste

Besides the above three analytic approaches to waste, scholars (Buendia, 1998; Drackner, 2005) have also explained waste from the societal perspective. Hereby, it is seen as a social reality, different according to societies, and represents a cultural and social value for the individuals in current and former societies. Since pre-industrial times, rural societies mainly produced easily assimilable and decomposable food, and durable goods based on natural raw materials (wood, leather, cotton, etc.). For these processes, those societies used little energy. Wastes generated in that way were scarce and easily recyclable: for example, leftover food for livestock feeding, agricultural remains, or animal excreta as manure to fertilise lands, etc. The concept of waste did not make any sense to those societies. It was mainly due to the scarcity of products and goods consumption at that time. Gradually, contemporary capitalism's logic of increasing production and mass consumption created a material by-product of waste and an environmental 'externality' of wasting (Fagan, 2003). Urban societies began to produce a great amount of waste difficult to recycle due to its quantity. These societies became net waste producers and were unable to recycle and give them back to their milieu without damaging it. Raw materials are considered non-finite, which causes the total amount of waste to be more than products. Wastes generated are composed of raw materials in different transformation grades, which have been transported from various remote sites, obtained from numerous difficult places especially minerals, and extracted in a very unnatural conditions. These processes imply an increasing energy cost and loss of soil productivity (Buendia, 1998). As these wastes are not given back to their original place nor recovered for ulterior use and are generated in large quantities, an economic model of limited duration had been established. Given the increasing waste generation, it is impossible to collect and treat them to diminish their danger, to recycle or deposit them risklessly. As a consequence, dumping enormous amounts of waste in the environment produces irreparable damage to ecosystems at a great scale affecting human health. There is a positive correlation between economic level of development and waste quantity (Buendia,1998). The higher the economic level, more waste is generated.

Ensuing risks of wastes and their disposal behaviour in India

Very few studies in contemporary sociology have attempted to theorise or acknowledge waste as a subject matter (O'Brien, 1999; Fagan, 2003). The discussion on their types and disposal behaviour of wastes is also negligible in the Indian context. Only a few studies (Borthakur and Govind, 2017, 2018; Raghu and Rodrigues, 2021) have exclusively problematised waste and discussed its disposal behaviour in detail. Borthakur and Govind (2017) draw scholars' attention towards the rising concern of electronic waste (e-waste) in the contemporary world due to globalisation, fast technological progress and innovations. A joint report by United Nations Environment Programme (UNEP, 2007) and United Nations University (UNU) predicted that by the year 2020, a growth of 500 per cent would be observed in India concerning e-waste from old computers. Borthakur and Govind (2017) indicate that e-waste accumulation is greatly influenced by people's disposal behaviour and associated awareness in India as well as at the global level. In contrast with developed countries, where products once rejected are considered 'waste' having no intrinsic value, 'waste' is considered valuable in developing countries. For instance, in India, people are reluctant to discard their useless electronics immediately without any financial incentive as e-waste is still considered a worthy commodity. Here electronic products often find different users before finally getting disposed of.

In terms of solid waste (SW) accumulation and disposal, Raghu and Rodrigues (2021) argue that due to technological advancement, population explosion, and consumer culture, both the quantity and quality of SW have changed. They also contend that illogical methods of waste disposal, increasing living standards of people, insufficient infrastructure, lack of resources, and slowly improving levels of sanitation have overburdened the waste disposal system, posing a huge challenge to designing a sustainable Solid Waste Management System. The study concludes that solid waste management behaviour in India is largely influenced by a set of factors namely, psychological factors (awareness of environmental knowledge and values), situational factors (convenience, opportunities), socioeconomic factors (income, age, and gender) and community factors (locality, distance to dumping sites).

Assuming waste as a social problem, sociologists have moved beyond an explanation of waste as a toxic threat to human beings and toward a more critical examination of waste as a reflection of socially constructed and historical relationships of power (Roby, 2016). An important study by German sociologist Ulrich Beck on risk is significant to understand how risk society functions. According to Beck, risks are embedded in modern industrial societies and are quite damaging yet ubiquitous (Beck, 1995). He affirms that risks follow a pattern of class inequality in modern societies and the social production of wealth is systematically accompanied by the social production of risks. While discussing ensuing risks due to waste in industrial society, Beck (2009) argues that the intensity of risk posed due to hazardous waste remains unknown. He defines risk as social constructions. The opaqueness of hazardous waste risk allows industry stakeholders and policymakers to elude accountability and get rid of critics. Such obscurity reproduces the existing power structure, so that profitable polluters are protected from their own hazardous waste outcomes while the masses are left to grapple with the risks (Beck, 2009).

Waste has a negative connotation concerning people's health and the environment. This is why the main effort is posed on hiding waste, on depositing it where it cannot be seen. Landfill is their answer to this problem. However, social opposition to landfills because of pollution and location difficulties, highlights the issue (Buendia, 1998). Waste management also becomes a profitable business. Recycling garbage to put materials again into the productive cycle is the current dominant model regarding waste. Waste minimisation, either by not producing it or by reusing it (which is different from recycling), has not received much social attention. As noted by Buendia (1998), resource productivity is the last of the new paradigms. It tries to resolve the contradiction between the social interest to increase wealth and the problem of both resource limits and harm to the environment produced by economic development. In contemporary time, where risks ensuing through the heap of waste/discard is on the rise, adequate research is required on waste from sociological perspective while taking into consideration the various psychological, behavioural, and situational factors which influence people's habits of wasting, recycling and disposal in developing nations.

Mahatma Gandhi's significant role in waste management

During India's struggle for Independence, Mahatma Gandhi was the most popular leader. Beside leading India to freedom, he was actively involved in various social causes including sanitation, personal hygiene, and cleanliness (Bandopadhyaya, 1964). Gandhian movement for sanitation started in South Africa during 1893 and continued till he was alive (1948). In his autobiography, he mentioned that Indians were careless in their habits and did not keep their house and surroundings clean. So he discussed the subject of sanitation and hygiene in different meetings. Gandhiji in South Africa (1893-1914) asked Indian settlers to overcome the whites' preconceptions against them in all areas of personal, home, and environmental cleanliness. In 1915 after returning to India, Gandhiji expressed serious interest in all the aspects of insanitation and lack of hygiene. Then he realised a need for educating people about sanitation, prevention of diseases, and untouchability (Anand, 2018; Rathi, 2014; Reddy and Gandhi, 1993; Sastry, 1933).

A noble initiative by the current Prime Minister (PM) of India, Narendra Damodardas Modi, has been initiation of a *Swachh Bharat Abhiyan* or Clean India Mission across the nation on the 150th birth anniversary of Mahatma Gandhiji in 2014. The Clean India Mission is targeted to achieve total eradication of open defecation, providing water supply, sanitation facility in villages and cities, and proper waste management by 2019 (Anand, 2018; Rathi, 2014). PM Narendra Modi has reminded all countrymen about the sanitation movement of Gandhiji, which has been inspired by the true feelings of patriotism. In addition to this, PM Modi has requested all Indians to pledge for taking their responsibility of cleanliness through a slogan '*na main gandagi karoonga, na main gandagi karne doonga*' meaning 'I shall not litter and won't allow anyone to do so' (Anand, 2018). Drawing from Gandhiji, PM Modi symbolises cleanliness by taking a broom and by cleaning the street to set the example in front of every Indian. It has been noted that untouchability and personal hygiene was the concern during the pre-independence time, where both the domains were acting as social evils of the Indian society. But, untouchability and personal hygiene are almost in a controllable situation for the present society. Currently, the real monster is Municipal Solid Waste (MSW).

Contextualising Gandhian perspective for waste management

Mahatma Gandhi's movement of sanitation also includes personal hygiene and clean surroundings. Gandhiji considered waste as a resource, and believed that leftover remains which cannot be used anymore should be managed scientifically. Hence, his waste management method can be applied under two sections, responsible consumption and self-management.

Responsible consumption for reduction in waste production: Gandhiji was very critical about the excessive indulgence of banquets and dresses specifically in Indian marriages and events. According to him, such extravaganza causes wastage of food and other materials. Specifically, the food waste are generated due to a customary or habitual practice amongst wealthy people. Also in rituals, ceremonies and banquets stored food and milk products get spoiled soon (CW, Vol. 83, 1981: 153, 220, 313, 365). All these symbolised the uncultured behaviour of people. At the same time, a massive amount of flowery decoration used in such occasions further increases the amount of organic waste (CW, Vol. 16, 1965: pp. 218, 219, 329).

In Ashram Notes, Gandhiji tried to sensualise the responsible consumption of resources. Such as, providing prior information to the Ashram mess authorities regarding their desire of skipping the meal, to avoid wastage of food and preserve raw materials for further usage. Not only this, he also propagated campaign against the uncultured behaviour of people during the banquet, especially the wealthy people. He stated that such activities can help to educate the public about responsible utilisation of social resource like consumption of food according to once hunger requirement to avoid leftovers. Replacing the flowery decoration from decorative garlands for any occasion can reduce the organic waste.

Self-management of waste produced: Gandhiji requested the refugees at the camps at Kurukshetra which were set up due to partition riots during 1947, to manage their waste by themselves. He believed that it is the responsibility of every human being to maintain cleanliness and self-scavenging. The collected work of Mahatma Gandhiji stated about a national conference of composting where Gandhiji supported Madeleine Slade (Mirabehn) at New Delhi, regarding the different forms of organic manure. It was contended that various organic waste such as human excreta, and cow dung can make good fertiliser for the agricultural fields. These manures can also be experimented by using slaughterhouse waste, sewage, sludge, agriculture waste, and yard waste. According to him, composting might be one of the appropriate ways to manage waste, as it would provide organic fertilisers to the fields. This is helpful to increase the yield, economically efficient and keeps the village clean. Such kind of self-management practices of waste must be performed in each village of the country.

During 1935, Gandhiji, explained about Dr G. I. Fowler's concept of 'Wealth and Waste' in weekly published journal *Harijan* on March 15, 1935. As per this concept human excreta from 300 million Indians are worth to obtain 600 million rupees annually. Likewise, the urinal disposal to manure fields can enhance the property of manure. Even animal dead bodies can be utilised to obtain nitrogen and phosphorus as an useful fertiliser for the fields. Gandhiji also communicated with '*Talimi Sangh*' members regarding the educational activities they performed at Sevagram during 1946. Besides that, he also discussed about the use of wastewater which has been creating a nuisance on the streets of the village. He suggested that the wastewater should be disposed into the water- requiring fields like vegetable beds and crop fields so that every drop of water can be utilised for greenery.

Application of the Gandhian method in waste management

As mentioned above, responsible consumption of resources and self-management of waste are the two pathways to make a waste management model applicable on the ground. For example, in the case of sustainable recycling model, the social gear can be understood by three sub-gears that are: (i) public health; (ii) sanitary workers' health; and (iii) public awareness which are mostly non-functional. This non-functional status of social gear may cause failure of sustainable recycling model in India. Hence, to make the gear functional, the Gandhian method of responsible consumption of resources and self-management of waste can be applied to these three sub-gears.

Application of responsible consumption

Public health: To make public health sub-gear functional, self-responsible consumption of resource can help to produce less amount of waste. Reduced quantity of waste which will spread less amount of disease causing pollutants and microorganisms.

Workers' health: The sanitary workers and rag pickers handle waste directly. In such a scenario their health is on the highest risk. Responsible consumption can also make responsible management that is the segregation of hazardous substances. Such responsible use of resources could ease out the way of waste handling for the workers and also secure their health.

Public awareness: Awareness among people can lead to responsible consumption. Whereas, responsible consumption can make people more aware of the processes of waste management. Responsible consumption can reduce the waste generated per capita. That would also reduce diseases associated with garbage and the burden of its control.

Application of self-management

Public health: The waste which has been generated need to be addressed soon so that its pollutants will not spread to cause any health hazard. In this case, organic waste can be managed through small kitchen composting. While inorganic waste can be segregated and sold to the small dealers.

Workers' health: When organic waste has been managed on a small scale, and segregated waste is available without more shuffling of waste, it will reduce the chances of accidents to the workers. Also, it would lower the risks of vector-borne diseases caused due to organic waste.

Public awareness: The per capita waste generation received per capita management lead to the development of habits and cleanliness culture or competition between people. This will help to create awareness of other communities too.

Hence, the Gandhian method can make social gear functional in India. The real requirement is to educate people, and realisation of rationality and accountability among them.

Research Design and Practice

Research design for this book has been developed through quantitative as well as qualitative methods supported by exhaustive review of literature to provide a robust solution to waste management problems of urban India. Data had been collected from primary and secondary sources by using different techniques. Primary data was collected from various sources such as, household surveys, interviews with different stakeholders, officials, Non Government Organisations (NGOs), members of civil society including doctors, young people who belong to age group of 10- 24 years. As well as data was also gathered from two different workshops which were conducted as part of the project "Waste Management Training to Reduce the Health Hazards of Solid Waste in Patna" at the Center for Energy and Environment, Indian Institute of Technology Patna, Bihar. The workshops were: Issues in Solid Waste Management,

October 11, 2014, and Effective Pedagogy for Waste Management, April 18, 2015. Secondary data sources for the study included Census of India, reports by CPCB, Annual Health Survey 2010-13. With help of various software, data were analysed.

Outline of the Book

The second chapter that sets the context of the discussion follows this introductory chapter. Exhaustive literature review forms the kernel of the third chapter. Literature is drawn from our transdisciplinary scholarship but the key guide is the research question at hand on waste. Thereafter, in chapter three, we zoom our comprehension on solid waste. Since we conducted our research in the region of Patna Municipal Corporation (PMC), we learnt about municipal solid waste and, therefore, delineate about them comprehensively. Chapter four makes public pedagogy pivotal. We think through educating our community of practice in the research locale to reduce the health hazards due to un-managed solid waste production. The last chapter of this book throws reflection and question that need to be pondered to make our world a better place to live. We have also dealt with the discard situation due to Covid pandemic. Dealing with what we construct as discard and how we treat discard is important. After all, it is not only about what we use and discard.

2

The Context of Discard Studies

Here and Now

Production is a social enterprise. To produce, we get into relationship with others in society. Production is sustained with re-production. It perpetuates inequality or precipitates change. These processes define our time and space. We analyse the nature of the wastes, the reasons for waste production, as well as the linkages of the local processes with global imperatives. We situate this study within the broader framework that locates environmental change with social change. It is certainly necessary and, complementary, to the focus on production and consumption that have been central to Sociology. Emphasis on waste, as Fagan (2003) indicates, is urgently needed as it is vital for understanding the relationship between social and environmental change.

While waste production is as old as human society, the nature of waste produced has changed with time. Earlier waste materials were from natural habitat or body parts of species. These wastes were mostly biodegradable. With time, the waste generated in our society has become more complex. Now, waste production is guided more by materialistic needs of people than subsistence livelihood practices. Industrial revolution has led to spurt of production and consumption that has been the key factor influencing an exponential rise in waste. The problem is accentuated in developing country like India. Here, the rapidly rising waste production is due to three interrelated factors, namely, high rates of population growth, rapid urbanisation, and a more sophisticated form of consumerism. On an average a resident in developing countries produce upto 0.79 kg of waste per capita per day (Hoornweg et al., 2012). The sources of these wastes include industrial, construction, biomedical, as well as municipal solid waste from households, hotels, resorts, restaurants, and other businesses. The waste, therefore, is composed of both organic and inorganic materials such as paper, soil, metal, plastics, glass, stone, wood, cardboard, textiles, and tires. Projections show that over the coming decades both per capita waste production rates and population size will increase, leading to even bigger challenges for relatively low income cities and countries, which currently contribute up to 35 per cent of the total waste production in the world (*ibid*).

Before we proceed with analysis of waste production, it is pertinent to define that in this book we focus only on solid waste which is defined as the unwanted or useless solid materials generated from combined residential, industrial and commercial activities in a given area. It may be categorised according to its origin (domestic, industrial, commercial, construction or institutional); according to its contents (organic material, glass, metal, plastic paper etc.) or according to hazard potential (toxic, non-toxin, flammable, radioactive, infectious etc.). Within various solid wastes, we specifically focus on Municipal Solid Waste (MSW) which is commercial and residential waste generated in municipal or municipal notified areas in either solid or semi-solid form excluding industrial hazardous wastes but including treatable bio-medical waste (The Municipal Solid Wastes Management and Handling Rules, 2000).

Environmental Protection Agency (EPA) has defined MSW as items which are utilised by humans and the remains of these used items that are thrown away (such as product packaging, grass clippings, furniture, clothing, bottles, food scraps, newspapers, appliances, paint, and batteries) more commonly called trash or garbage and is generated in municipal notified areas (USEPA, 2012).

Table 1 explains the various generators and types of solid wastes. As evident from the table, MSW is both commercial and residential waste as they originate from different sources like houses, schools, restaurants, markets, institutions, and businesses. Though MSW is a worldwide problem yet its adverse implications are enormous in developing countries.

Table 1: Generators and Types of Solid Waste

Source	Typical Waste Generators	Types of Solid Waste
Residential	Single and multifamily dwellings	Food wastes, paper, cardboard, plastics, textiles, leather, yard wastes, wood, glass, metals, ashes, special wastes (e.g., bulky items, consumer electronics, white goods, batteries, oil, tires), and household hazardous wastes (e.g., paints, aerosols, gas tanks, waste containing mercury, motor oil, cleaning agents), e-wastes (e.g., computers, phones, TVs)
Commercial	Stores, hotels, restaurants, markets, office buildings	Paper, cardboard, plastics, wood, food wastes, glass, metals, special wastes, hazardous wastes, e-wastes
Institutional	Schools, hospitals(non-medical waste), prisons, government buildings, airports	Same as commercial
Construction and Demolition	New construction sites, road repairs, renovation sites, demolition of buildings	Wood, steel, concrete, dirt, bricks, tiles

Source: Adapted from World Bank Report, 1999.

Various studies (Huntley, 2010) have noted that MSW are the most difficult sources of solid waste to manage because of its diverse range of composite materials. A considerable portion of these wastes consists of organic matters resulting from the preparation and consumption of food, including vegetable peelings and leftover food. It also consists of plastics, paper, glass, textiles, cellophane, metals and some hazardous waste from household products such as paint, garden pesticides, pharmaceuticals, fluorescent tubes, personal care products, batteries containing heavy metals and discarded wood treated with dangerous substances such as anti-fungal and anti-termite chemicals. In the recent past there has been an increased focus to address issues related to solid waste management in developing countries, especially in terms of methods of disposal, recycling and treatment of waste. However, none of the studies till date have accounted for the factors that lead to production of waste as practices of everyday lifestyle within a specific socio-cultural milieu.

We contend that MSW generations are result of practices of everyday life. Therefore, MSW management is a complex issue due to changing lifestyle of people, rapid urbanisation, and under-estimated contributors and stakeholders (Jha et al., 2011). Developing countries are characterised by expanding industrial and service sectors leading to rapid urbanisation and increasing rate of rural to urban migration. Raj and Raj (2015, 2018) argue that Patna is no exception to the phenomena of urbanisation and that this has altered the relationship to the patterns of consumption and thereby nature of MSW generation. The production of MSW as suggested by Raj and Singh (2017) has an association with the changing consumption patterns in cities where consumption has become a mode of lifestyle practice. Kaushal et al., (2012) and Singh et al., (2014) in their studies suggest thereby that this has led to highlighting of the missing link between the MSW generation and its management.

Our research illustrates that the rate of solid waste generation is more a functional result of our social activities. As noted earlier, one of the major sources of MSW generations is the households. In here, family is the primary unit of socialisation where individuals develop their understanding of 'what are wastes'. Learning and formation of basic habits forms the kernel of our social practices. This encompasses daily dietary practices including preparation and consumption of food. They also comprise of leisure activities, customs, rituals, hobbies, and other lifestyle choices. These everyday practices are co-related with our environmental practices as their manifest or latent functions effect our environment. Hoornweg et al. (2012) indicate that waste composition and production are related to factors, such as, culture, climate, and state of development. Moreover, Sharan (2006) contends that environment is a fluid concept, linking cultures, populations, materials and spaces in specific ways in particular historical conjunctures.

It has been noted that per unit percentage increase in population and income leads to 1.04 per cent and 0.34 per cent increase in MSW generation per capita, respectively (Johnstone et al., 2004; Dyson et al., 2005). Economic growth is also related to environmental degradation as its relationship follows the pattern of the Environmental Kuznets Curve (EKC). Stern (2004) defines EKC as the indicators of environmental degradation, which rise in the first phase and then starts to fall with increasing per capita income. He further argues that developing countries are presently in the first phase of EKC witnessing the parallel environmental degradation and pollution rise (Stern, 2004). Developing countries are facing a serious issue of rapid increase in MSW generation rate and their growing economy is unable to support basic services to manage the large volume of MSW on daily basis (Minghua et al., 2009; Raj and Raj, 2015). As a result, the collected MSW is dumped in open areas at landfilling sites while the uncollected MSW remain strewn on the roadside, many-a-time clogging drainage. Such unsafe and inadequate management of MSW put the environment, human, and animal health at risk (Zurbrugg, 2003). MSW causes serious environmental risks, which ascends further due to the transfer of MSW pollutants into the soil, water, and air. The pollution rises because of MSW, which gives rise to direct and indirect health risks to the population of the city. Sanitary workers and rag pickers are more prone to health risks because of their direct contact with MSW. Harmful chemicals and gaseous emissions from MSW during its management processes lead to the emergence of greater health risks. Besides, health of the population is also adversely affected due to breeding of disease-causing vectors, like flies, rodents, chemical compounds, and toxic gases. Developmental and social processes such as industrialisation, urbanisation, rising

MSW, lack of MSWM triggers environment degradation and results in serious health hazards. Raj and Raj (2015) have listed several sources, major generators and the type of MSW produced by these such as- residential localities, commercial areas, institutional and construction sites. These sources belong to families, hotels, markets, schools and construction sites. As the MSW generator's lifestyle and consuming pattern changes along with rapid urbanisation it leads to the exponential increase in the amount of MSW and variation in its composition (Pandey, 2014; Raj and Raj, 2015).

Lifestyle and Waste

Lifestyles refer to specific forms in which individuals live and interpret their lives in a social context. To portray lifestyle from a macro-perspective three core dimensions have to be combined: social status or class; attitudes and preferences; and behaviour (Bello, 2018; Reusswig et al., 2018). These dimensions have a significant impact on the level of waste generated in a particular household. The ongoing changes in the economic situation also resulted in a sharp increase in rural-urban migration with a consequent increase in urban solid waste (Bello, 2018). According to Zafar (2016), lavish lifestyles, ineffective legislation, infrastructural challenges, unconcerned attitude and lack of environmental awareness are the primary factors leading to the growing waste management problem in the Middle East. Advanced living standards coupled with the lack of waste collection and disposal facilities have transformed these wastes into a liability. By stressing the youth segment, scholars (Mondejar–Jiménez et al., 2016) identified three main actions for preventing food waste, namely, consuming household leftovers, understanding the date labels on food, and planning food purchases. Further, leftovers are usually considered one of the main reasons for discarding food (Williams et al., 2012). Therefore, investigating ways to recover and reuse food could certainly mitigate the waste phenomenon (Quested et al., 2013). Similarly, the ability to check food stocks before shopping and to follow a shopping list can reduce the probability that food becomes spoiled and is thrown away (Mondéjar-Jiménez et al., 2016). Finally, attention toward date labels could help consumers to make more informed food purchases and consumption (Mirghotbi and Pourvali, 2013). Several scholars (Parizeau et al., 2015; Hebrok and Boks, 2017) found a positive relationship between household lifestyles and food waste production. A study by Savelli (2020) demonstrates that food waste preventive behaviours are negatively related to food waste intensity, as established through previous research.

Categories of Waste Produced

Food is the first category. It is one of the most common items of consumption that is directly related to waste production. Apart from what we eat, food involves various other aspects that acquire meaning and significance when examined from the perspectives of waste generation. To start with common sense rationality influences the selection of different foods. For example, during fieldwork many of our respondents pointed that they would prefer to buy the vegetables from a specific outlets that sells the vegetables in plastic bags properly labelled with price and weight rather than common vendors where one needs to bargain and where even the vegetables are not properly packed.

Most of the families surveyed for this research are nuclear families and often have double income. In such a situation they lead a very busy life. Also due to availability of large amount of disposable incomes, these families tend to engage in eating out more often. Events of eating out in urban centres of India does not necessarily mean dining at restaurants rather people also prefer to buy fast food from street vendors and small eating joints at the road side. Foods at these joints are served either in aluminium or thermocal plates, which are easily disposable after use but not degradable. Large portions of MSW that are littered on roads in many cities in India are composed of such items. Interestingly, almost all the small restaurants in every city offer 'free home delivery services' which have become very popular, as one gets to enjoy restaurant food at home without having to physically travel. Such practices have become more common and convenient during and after the Covid pandemic. All these foods are served in aluminium foiled packets in a plastic bag and accompanied by a latest menu card of the restaurant along with paper napkins, plastic spoon or forks, and pouches of sauce or salad. This practice is not environmental friendly and becomes a big part of the daily waste production at household level.

More than 70 per cent of the respondents stated that on an average the intake of non home-made food is approximately three times a week. Most residents have a competition with those who live in other apartments of the building or with those in the neighbourhood about their cool lifestyle including the practice of eating out. This is quite an alarming rate of consumption generating huge amount of waste. As Baudrillard (1998) depicts these are consumptions of 'signs' to reinforce a specific social status. Respondents were given option as to whether they would prefer food to be served in steel or other metal utensils which could be washed and re-used. All of them replied they would not prefer such arrangements as they feel it might not be hygienic. They also gave examples, why they choose certain restaurants over other for home delivery mainly because of their "hygienic packaging". Then respondents were asked whether they are aware of the environmental effects of using such products, all of them gave an affirmative reply but when they were enquired as to what could be done to minimise production of waste none replied that they should check their levels of consumption. Rather everyone blamed the municipal authority for not implementing better pick up and transport facilities of solid waste.

Waste generation from food consumption is not only limited at household level but also at the source where food is sold. Here, the roads are infested with numerous eating joints and vendors selling various types of fast food at different price ranges affordable by people of all income groups. Based on participant observation in various cities, it was noticed that in the evening time the sale of such fast food items increases and the consumers are mostly young adults. There is an increasing trend in India for young people to attend academic coaching classes. Most of such classes are held after school or college hours in the evening. This provides a specific type of socialisation among young adults, who hang out after the classes at the road side eating joints. These eating vendors provide a particular space for interaction among young people where along with food they also enjoy the company of their friends. Under these circumstances, consumption of food is more an act to establish a social identity amongst a peer group. However, such consumption practices are a major cause of generating huge amount of solid waste in the region, characterised by "use and throw" plates, cups, glass, spoon and napkins.

Electrical appliances and gazettes are the next category.In developing countries due to the widespread availability of electrical and electronic goods, there has been a tremendous increase in amount of e-waste which has become a serious environmental concern (Pandey and Govind, 2014). These electrical goods range between toys; personal care items (such as hair drier, electrical razor); entertainment and/educational products (television, video and CD players, i-pads, laptops, computers, tablets, and mobile phones) and appliances that are used for household chores and activities, for example, washing machines, microwave machines, toaster, mixer-grinder, and so on. All the households surveyed for the study reported of having these products, though the quantity and brand varied. One of the respondents replied "these days we have become so used to these appliances, like washing machine and microwave that it is impossible to think of a life without these". Another respondent stated that "...at times I wonder earlier how we managed our lives without cell phones (laughs). I mean now it is so much easier to stay connected with your friends all the time."

When we asked the respondents whether they were aware that such items generate huge amount of e-waste and the adverse effect they have on the environment, their responses were interesting. About 43 per cent said that they were aware about e-waste but not specifically about environmental hazards caused by them; while 26 per cent reported they thought only computers and laptops produce e-waste; 19 per cent stated they were not sure about how everyday use of electrical appliances can produce e-waste and the environmental effects were limited only to those who deal with these wastes; and only 12 per cent expressed concern about reducing e-waste production. Respondents were given option that if they were willing to use less of these products to minimise e-waste production, their responses were almost anonymous as they stated that one has to lose something for enjoying comforts in life. From in-depth interviews it was evident that the purposes of these goods are as means of communication to express identity and mark status (Stillman, 2003). Lodziak (2002) suggests that nowadays sources of identity dwell in the world of images, symbols and signs. Giddens (1991) thus observes that a new kind of consumer had emerged for whom consumption itself plays a central role in constructing new senses of identity based on and around the possession and ownership of status-conferring goods.

Not far behind we have the category that covers **personal care products and sanitary items.** A large proportion of the MSW comprises of personal care items, such as cosmetics, deodorants, diapers, and so on. There has been an increase in consumption of these items whose values and comforts are being reinforced through daily advertisements in the media. In every household these items are very common. In fact, from the survey it was evident that the levels of consumption of these products are almost at par with the household's consumption of grocery items. For example, about 87 per cent of the respondents reported that they buy such products of personal care more than twice every month. This suggests the frequent use of these items. Bourdieu (2003) argues that consumption is the articulation of a sense of identity. According to him our identity is made up by our consumption of goods, which displays our expression of taste. Many people's sense of identities then, are affirmed and contested through specific acts of consumption (Jackson and Thrift, 1995). People define themselves by what they buy and by the meaning that they give to the goods and services that they acquire. Lodziak (2002: 51) argues that - for those with the financial means - there exists a "self-identity industry" that includes health-clubs, fitness gyms, therapy centres, beauty salons, cosmetic surgeries and use of specific products. The same is true for the respondents of this study. They all agreed that their consumption of particular personal care items were influenced more by advertisements to forge a distinct personal identity which is characterised by living a comfortable lifestyle. To illustrate this with an example from another context, and as reported by Colon et al. (2013), all households that had children below three years of age uses diapers for them but unfortunately these diapers are not disposed off in a sanitarily hygienic manner causing adverse environmental affects.

Real estate is another significant category in most of the urban centres these days. As mentioned earlier, a large amount of MSW is also produced through construction and demolition. A tour of any urban centre illustrates that new buildings and shopping complexes, including malls, are being constructed in various places. With a rise in disposable income among the middle class as well as easy availability of various home loan schemes provided by the banks, urban India has witnessed a steady rise in the real estate market. Another factor that adds to this real estate boom can be contributed to the opening of different offices and state head quarters of various NGOs. Almost 35 per cent of the household surveyed lived in house and/ apartment which they owned while the rest 65 per cent lived in rental accommodation. Those who lived in rental accommodation, approximately 85 per cent of them mentioned that they have pre-booked apartment, which was under construction. 72 per cent of those who lived in their own house reported they plan to have some construction in their premises for commercial uses. This could be either to rent it as office space or else open student accommodation. Interestingly, all the respondents were aware that such activities would generate a lot of solid waste, but to them the attraction of income superseded their concern for environment. All these imply that apart from consumption of products to reinstate their social status, people in urban India also indulged in consumption of space (Jackson and Thrift, 1995) which is also responsible for generating solid waste in these cities.

Transport vehicles can be an environmental problem and an arena in which consumers are both the senders and receivers of symbolic meaning. By choosing to cycle or by selecting one rather than another type of car, individuals convey information about themselves. This is just as they interpret the social meaning of 'other' transport practices. Transport vehicles are important in connecting people between different spatial locations. Population growth in these cities is accompanied by growth of transport vehicles as well. Among these, the number of personal transport vehicles is ever increasing. Easy loans from different banks serve as a lubricant. However, it is the family's competition to have better car than the neighbour that sets the process. Having an expensive car is a conventional symbol of high social status all over the world. The roads here are unable to support the increasing number of vehicles-resulting in traffic congestion. Also, while new cars have taken to the road, old means of transport are still there. Animal driven cart or human driven rickshaw or slow moving tractor adds to the slow traffic situation and ever increasing sound and air pollution. What concerns us here in this book is solid waste. We have found a correlation between a stand-still traffic and disposal of waste in the city by people using transport vehicles to connect between two spatial locations. Participant observation at select traffic points show that throwing of wrappers and other left over from a car rises with increasing traffic congestion. Participant observation also guides us to comprehend the consumption pattern here, and thereby, waste production reflects a complex admixture of tradition and modernity. We will discuss these and other significant points after we have delineated the consumption pattern and waste production below.

Consumption Patterns and Waste Production

Consumption is a multi-dimensional concept. Its definitions vary according to the academic discipline by which it is perceived. For example, sociologists have focused on consumption as a social activity rather than as a pure economic activity (Bocock, 1993). Once people are influenced by the social and cultural practices associated with the ideology of current day consumerism stemming from westoxicated values, then even if they cannot afford to buy the goods portrayed in films, advertising, and in the media, they still desire them. Consumption is, therefore, seen as being based increasingly upon desires, not simply upon need (Baudrillard, 1998). This sows the seed for analysing an exceptional form of consumer behaviour termed *conspicuous consumption*. Mason (1983:3) distinguishes it as "being motivated by a desire to impress others with the ability to pay particular high prices for prestige products." He, further, asserts that it is a form of consumption which is inspired by social rather than by the economic or physiological utility of products. Conspicuous consumption is not a recent phenomenon although it may be in a new *avatar* in India. This concept surfaced as early as 1899 when Veblen (1992), in his seminal work *The Theory of the Leisure Class*, mentioned such consumption behaviour. Veblen contends that wealthy individuals often consume conspicuous goods and services in order to advertise their wealth and thereby achieve greater status. Hence, in conspicuous consumption the commodities consumed are not necessities. They are 'status goods' or 'positional goods'. According to Baudrillard (1998) such goods are 'signs' or 'sign values' as well as images or messages rather than commodities that are consumed. The purposes of these goods are as means of communication to express identity and mark status (Stillman, 2003). Thus, conspicuous consumption feeds off a status system (Mason, 1981). Categories of waste produced in urban India, and as discussed in the section above, justify this pattern of consumption.

When Veblen proposed his theory of conspicuous consumption it was designed as a concept applicable only to the rich and wealthy class, but in the postmodern society, often termed the 'consumer society' (Clarke, 2003), conspicuous consumption is one of the most dominant features of the new middle class. As Mason (1981: 150) states, "...conspicuous consumption may well be confirmed in future as an exclusively middle class form of behaviour". Ger and Belk (1996: 272) have added "consumptionscape" to Appadurai's initial five scapes (ethnoscapes, mediascapes, technoscapes, financescapes and ideoscapes) that have defined global cultural flows and disjunctures (Appadurai, 2003) and have tried to explain recent global flows of consumption. They state that the global consumptionscape adds to the resources available to people and becomes part of how consumers draw from all available global and local, new and old sources, as they use products to position themselves in local age, gender, social class, religion and ethnic hierarchies. Based on this, Kjeldgaard (2003), situates consumption behaviour within the broader perspective of the global-local nexus, and explains how relations of a particular 'local' with the global cultural economy affect consumption behaviour. Being cool and hanging out may signify global flow, but consuming *golgappa* (a popular street food in India) at a street corner gives a local flavour.

Bocock (1993) asserts that modern patterns of consumption for urban dwellers are, in part, a result of living in the metropolis, the city and its suburbs. The processes involved of living in an urban location increase the awareness of style, of the need to consume within a repertory which is both distinctive to a social group and expressive of individual preferences. Ger (1999) states that in transitional societies they also face tensions in their attempt to face the future (modernity, progress) rather than the past (poor, rural, backwards, traditional) whilst maintaining their roots and habits. Day in, day out, practices reflect the negotiation of what it is to be modern, to be sensible and thrifty whilst demonstrating success and respectability, and so on. Their argument can be supported by the patterns of conspicuous consumption among urban middle class in India. Easy availability and accessibility of materials to the middle class population in cities allows this group of people to imitate the consumerist values of the west disregarding their traditional behaviour. This, we believe, is noteworthy cause of increasing waste generation.

The everyday practices, daily habits, and routine activities can be understood within the framework of acculturalisation and deculturisation (Raj and Raj, 2004). These two processes always go hand-in-hand and never occur in isolation. First step involves getting comfortable in usage of packaged products (acculturisation) thus detaching from earlier ethics of re-use (deculturisation). The effect on behavioural changes is not what we intent to analyse here. Rather, we are interested in what happens after being effected by such changes. We believe that once the process of deculturisation gets established, the desiring machine (Deleuze and Guattari, 2005) has greatest discomfort when not using these products. The meaning of an object, like a car or organic foods, or a practice such as biking, reflects perceptions and judgements about how and in what ways it differs from or is similar to alternatives, and where, when, how, and by whom it is owned, consumed, or engaged in. Desire gets introduced into thought, discourse, and then into action.

Consumption pattern of food and the kind of waste generated around it leads us to situate the behaviour as hedonism. Packaged food points to an experience of enjoyment. It means that you eat exactly what you want and when you want it. Hedonism can also take an environmental form, as when consumers view the consumption of packaged food as a sensual treat and take pleasure in the experience or at least the association of better quality, taste, and texture. This might be a case that women who spent more time in kitchen preparing food are now busy. *Being busy* is a sign of having an active and time-scheduled daily life. This is a context where shopping and cooking are designed not to take up too much time. Hence, semi-manufactured goods seem to be necessary. The proliferation of processed foods promises *emancipation from household chores* especially for women. Media and advertising reinforce these symbolic meanings. Moreover, *signs of being modern and western* are important especially in India. Processed foods are associated with a sense of decency and self-respect that comes from not depriving ones family of the good life as seen on TV or as lived by ones more affluent neighbours. All such foods are available at the supermarkets in plastic, tin or aluminium packets. Though it is easy to prepare and consume these food items but unfortunately their packaging materials are neither bio-degradable nor recyclable. As per the Municipal Solid Waste Handling Rule (2000) the minimum time taken for tin and aluminium to degrade is between 100-500 years, while it is one million years for plastic.

It is cultural practice, then, and the knowledge production mechanism that is at the root of the problem. Rapid material and technological growth gave rise to a cultural modernisation with materialism and consumerism at the core. A common theme which emerges from all these cases is the changing definition of what it is to be modern. Throughout, the pattern is one in which the life which people aspire to or expect relies on an increasing number of appliances and environmentally problematic services relating to mobility, hygiene, and increasing standards of indoor comfort. The availability of these services and the technologies which make them possible symbolise modernity. This modernity is the yardstick for normality. Any deviance, either through inability of economic or cultural capital, desires enforcement for achieving normality. Consumers have their own yardsticks with which they measure levels and patterns of sufficient consumption. The moving mark of what is enough and pleasurable is negotiated in moral terms. Consumers legitimise their own high levels or aspirations of personal consumption with reference to a repertoire of justifications and excuses. Justifications include pleasure, connoisseurship, instrumentalism, or altruism while excuses tend to focus on external forces, including arguments about the way of the modern world, or the need to make up for past deprivation, or to reward success. Paradoxically, the prevalence of these defensive vocabularies highlights the extent to which the ethos of consumption is legitimised.

The process of knowledge production and appropriation is led by the presiding deities of European enlightenment. Dualism leads the way. Either you are good or you are bad. Your modernity may be de-contextual, but you must aspire to be one. Formalistic knowledge production trajectories give emphasis to the Newtonian, Baconian, and Cartesian rationality. It is rooted in everything we produce and consume. This monocultural rationality negates local context as well as environmental concerns. Also, environmentalism in India has only been mild and controlled by the modernized elite, several budding environmentalists have been integrated into environmental departments in universities and in government agencies and municipalities. Such institutionalisation and professionalisation fostered a consensus-oriented form of environmentalism within the wider society. This background helps explain the proliferation of government initiated programmes for citizen participation in local environmental improvements, new non-radical, professional environmental organisations and a growth in environmental journalism in the mass media.

In the above section, we have tried to connect the missing lines between consumption pattern and waste production. This could be pertinent to comprehend the nature and type of waste produced, especially municipal solid waste. We have seen that it is the misplaced and raging consumption pattern that goes for increasing waste production. The 'positivistic' knowledge machine only justifies the conspicuous consumption and has become part of way of life of people in places like Patna and such other urban centres in India. In the next section, we would like to examine what re-enforces these patterns especially in our research site. We start with precise discussion on globalisation.

G-local-isation and Lumpenism

The term globalisation is used by various groups, often loosely, and thus assumes various meanings. Typically, globalisation is described as increased economic, cultural, environmental and social interdependencies, along with new transnational financial and political formations, arising out of the increasing mobility of capital, labour and information, with both homogenising and differentiating tendencies (Mittelman, 2001). Appadurai (1999) rightly states, the word 'globalisation' provokes heated reactions. Some of these reactions concern definitions, others concern whether globalisation has 'gone too far' or not, and still others are about the officialisation of the term and its conversion into a slogan for the forces that support liberalisation, marketisation and reform across the world. Sociologist Robertson's (1992) explanation of globalisation is based on the theory of society as a specific kind of social system. He states that globalisation at the cultural level began to occur because of two things *compression of the world* and *global consciousness*. Kellner (2000) asserts that the term globalisation is a theoretical construct and argues that the concept entails everything from the westernisation of the world to the ascendancy of capitalism. He concludes that globalisation is one of the main processes noted in modern and post-modern social theories. By analysing the various views of globalisation held by people in developed countries Kellner demonstrates that while some people view globalisation as increasing the homogeneity of societies, others on the contrary, view globalisation as increasing the hybridisation of cultures and diversity.

In this book, it is not our intent to engage into a detailed discussion about globalisation, rather we would like to reflect upon how the process of globalisation is responsible for the rise of a new middle class which is characterised by specific consumption practices leading to increased intensity of waste generation in developing countries. Globalisation takes local roots here and can be comprehended as glocalisation, especially in the manner it implicates the class structure. We believe that the growth of middle class in urban India is based on a pattern where lumpensim as a cultural practice has been the harbinger of social change. Through history the notion of the middle class has remained highly contentious in the social sciences. The liberal pluralists tend to regard the middle class as primarily a cultural entity defined by values of individualism and rationality, as well as by indicators of status, occupation and income. Accordingly, the middle class cannot be distinguished from the bourgeoisie and there is no means of distinguishing between the type of social power that they derive from property on the one hand, and salaries and qualifications on the other. However, while scholars continue to struggle to provide a comprehensive definition of the middle class, there has emerged in the literature a sub-group within this class, namely the *new middle class*. This conceptual framework originates in opposition to the official Marxist theories of the late nineteenth century. Betz (1992) relates the growth of the new middle class with changing production systems in a society and analyses it against a postmodern background. Betz (*ibid*.: 100) points that the "the theoretical approaches to describe the new middle class in post-industrial, consumer and information society generally characterise the new middle class as a rather homogenous class (the service class of employers, managers and professionals) united in its members' shared pursuit of social status." He argues that based on this theorisation, the new middle class emerges at a particular stage in a country's economic development where its precise function is to promote consumption ethics. In the present context we contend that globalisation has generated substantial employment in a number of developing countries like India. This in turn has given birth to a new urban middle class in these countries. An important majority of the members of this emerging class are employed in the service sector and constitute a growing and increasingly large proportion of these countries populations (Shurmer-Smith, 2000).

Betz (1992: 99) concludes that the new middle class is intricately connected to the growth of the "societe de consommation." Featherstone (1987) states that consumption and tastes become vital channels in the struggle between various classes and a particular class, the new middle class, is formed leading to a growing aestheticisation of everyday life via signs, symbols, and images of pleasure for consumption. Hence, the very nature of the new middle class puts heavy emphasis on consumption. In such a situation the new middle class are the 'new heroes of consumer culture'. In developing Asian countries, with economies predominantly based on extensive agriculture, the new middle class did not gain prominence either in number or in interest among researchers, media or politicians due to their insignificant numbers until the 1970s. From that decade onwards globalisation trends triggered a range of liberalisation policies across Asia (albeit to very different degrees and not in Burma) causing a shift in many occupational structures and the rapid growth of export-focused industries leading to an employment boom.

In Asia the term 'new rich' is used interchangeably with 'new middle class'. This term is used to describe in broad terms the new wealthy social groups that have emerged from industrial changes in Asia, with their social power based either on capital and expertise or rent and/or position in the extensive state apparatus (Gerke, 2000). The new rich are thus the professional middle class. Nonetheless, this term is a starting point for examination rather than an analytical tool. This needs to be clarified because the new rich is neither a cohesive category nor does it have common historical roots, and its impacts vary from one country to another depending on the pattern of economic transition in the country. Therefore, there are likely to be several patterns in the emergence of the new rich and its influence on the cultural, social, economic and political life of the country under study (Robinson and Goodman, 1996). This group is commonly characterised by a newly emerging lifestyle - a metropolitan, or *nouveau riche* lifestyle - in which the consumption of items such as brand name clothes, personal adornments and expensive pleasurable pursuits has become central (Bocock, 1993). In this book we suggest that changing consumption patterns is directly linked to their change in lifestyle which has impacted upon the production of waste in these cities.

The new rich in India are a product of lumpenism. Lumpen way of life was epitomised during the last few decades when the agrarian and rural classes became the dominant caste. The unequal utilisation of resources by the previous regimes, mainly led by upper caste, was rightly resented and giving back was purposely engulfed in behaviour patterns not appreciated by the upper echelon. Investment in infrastructure was stopped as the institutions were so designed, by the earlier political administration, that the benefits would be utilised only by the established classes. For example, cities like Patna, pathetically, became a victim of its own people who in trying to get back to each other took resort in unruly behaviour that can at best be classified as lumpensim. Ascertain of this behaviour patterns was visible in every walk of life. The political class enjoyed the benefits while the rot only stemmed further. The bureaucracy resented but was only concerned with their immediate neighbourhood. The bureaucracy encompassed more funds through increasing corrupt practices. The flow of funds in the market for unparallel consumerism has direct co-relation with corruption in most branches of the bureaucracy here. The boom in real estate is also helped with incomparable extortion of funds by the lumpen political class and the corrupt bureaucracy. These two are joined by the expatriate of that province, especially those who have made a mark for themselves in other local in India. However, the spurt in consumerist behaviour is a gift from them as well.

Use of lumpenism to comprehend the social formation and cultural patterns in urban India may draw from but is not directly related to the concept of lumpen bourgeoise espoused by A.G. Frank (1972). However, like the class discussed by Frank, even the culture of the class in urban India is insensitive to the local need. Whether it is the condition of pollution in the river Ganga or the streets, people are only bothered about themselves and their loved ones. They are insensitive to the community and their environment. They learn from practices of the other culture(s) and try their best to catch up to it. But, when it comes to the practices which sustained their own environment, people feel that by continuing those practices they may not be considered modern. The local word here for adopting the so called modern practice is *vikashit* which in English would mean developed. But, as one elderly respondent concluded, this attitude shows *vikrit* (meaning, that which has lost its mainstay) mentality. Overt rowdiness has been curbed during the current political regime but insensitivity and an attitude of communal ownership is missing. While living rooms should be clean, but there is no concern for the streets and the way inappropriate disposal of waste can create different kinds of health hazard, for instance.

3

Conceptualising Solid Waste

This chapter provides a detailed sketch of previous research on the topic in various sections, namely: Municipal Solid Waste Management (MSWM) policies; MSWM and its challenges; MSWM and public health; Integrated Sustainable Solid Waste Management (ISSWM); and finally the research gaps. The section on MSWM and its challenges have been divided further into subsections termed as: MSW generation and composition; MSW collection and transportation; MSW processing and recovery; MSW treatment and disposal; and public awareness among various stakeholders.

Municipal Solid Waste Management Policies

In 1990, for the first time the critical situation of MSW was reported in India when a huge number of public complaints were registered against the unscientific practices of MSWM (Gupta, 2010). Thereafter in 1996, the Indian Supreme Court ordered the Ministry of Environment and Forests (MoEF), Government of India, to develop MSWM rules. In 2000, rulebook named *Municipal Solid Waste (Management and Handling) Rules* was released to all urban local bodies. For the sake of public health and environmental protection interest MoEF, Government of India released the revised draft of *Municipal Solid Waste (Management and Handling) Rules* (2013) which aimed to address all significant features of MSWM such as, improved institutional approaches and planning, engaging technical experts, institutional and organisation involvement, financial and legal dimensions (MoEF, 2013). This draft had been opened for suggestions and clarifications as various serious aspects of MSWM was missing in it. MSW stakeholder's one major disagreement has been to have separate rules for construction and demolition waste which were still a part of *Municipal Solid Waste (Management and Handling) Rules*, 2013 and 2014 (Agarwal et al., 2015). This objection sustains in the revised notification of *Solid Waste Management Rules*, 2015 published under the Ministry of Environment, Forest and Climate Change (MoEFCC), Government of India. When opened for public opinion, on 3rd June 2015 the immediate action was requested on rulebook formation for construction and demolition waste (MoEFCC, 2015). Finally, the Government of India duly considered it, and a separate rule book namely *Construction and Demolition Waste Management Rules*, (2016) was released on 29 March 2016. Soon on 8th April 2016, it was again revised with considerable changes and named *Solid Waste Management Rules,* 2016 (MoEFCC, 2016).

Apart from these rules passed in 2016, various other rules related to different facts of wastes were also simultaneously formed. For example, *Non-biodegradable Garbage (Control) Ordinance*, (2006), *Plastic Waste Management Rules*, 2016 amended and now known as *Plastic Waste Management (Amendment) Rules*, 2018 (MoEFCC, 2018). The MoEFCC has constitutionalised the *Solid Waste Management Rules*, (2016) as a nationwide policy. It states that to manage urban MSW every municipality has to follow the practices explained in these rules, as it provides a guideline to them (MoEFCC, 2016). Some other documented policies related to MSWM are the Report of National Plastic Waste Management Task Force (August, 1997), the Supreme Court appointed Burman Committee's Report (March, 1999), and the Ministry of Urban Affairs' Shukla Committee's Report (January, 2000) (Singh and Raj, 2018). Another important programme introduced on 2nd October 2014 on the 150th birth anniversary of the father of the nation Mahatma Gandhi, by the Ministry of Urban Development

(MoUD), is "*Swachh Bharat Abhiyan*". The current Prime Minister (PM) of India, Narendra Modi, has initiated a Clean India Mission across the nation. This mission is a national campaign to promote cleanliness. It also encompasses MSWM. Local government is supposed to emphasise on social priorities and consequences that explain the purpose and implications of this mission (Agarwal et al., 2015; Anand, 2018).

A review of the existing rules regarding MSW reveals that social inference, economic implication, and environmental protection from MSWM - the three bottom lines of sustainability have not been sufficiently addressed in the current rules/guidelines. Public behaviour, awareness, and health safety are not legally framed in the currently followed policies. For cities in India the most accessible sustainable option is recycling as it can generate employment for urban poor without much investment (Kaseva and Gupta, 1996). It can also preserve natural resources indirectly (Hoornweg and Bhada-Tata, 2012). Public awareness, behavioural changes, and creating awareness regarding health safety can make recycling sustainable (Vij, 2012).

Municipal Solid Waste Management and its Challenges

MSWM encompasses various processes such as proper planning, policies, socio-economic conditions, climatic suitability, storage, collection, transportation, treatment, final disposal, and monitoring (Tchobanoglous et al., 1993; Hoornweg and Bhada-Tata, 2012). MSWM sector follows an accepted hierarchy, the earliest known usage of the 'waste management hierarchy' appears to be Ontario's Pollution Probe in the early 1970s. This hierarchy proposed 'Three Rs' technology (reduce, reuse, recycle) which are placed at top of the hierarchy but now a fourth R (recovery) is added (Hoornweg and Bhada-Tata, 2012). According to Ontario's Pollution Probe report, hierarchy also depends upon the financial, environmental, social, and management factors followed by a particular country (Sincero and Sincero, 1996). It is suggested that integration of these elements along with amendment in policies and technology from time to time can make MSWM successful and sustainable. From the literature review such as Sharholy et al., (2008); Shekdar, (2009); Hoornweg and Bhada-Tata, (2012); Tchobanoglous et al., (2014), it is evident that major challenges of MSWM in developing countries are generation of large volume of MSW and inadequate methods for MSWM. In these countries the responsibilities and budget allocation for MSWM both are within the purview of municipal authorities (Singh et al., 2012). Though large expenditure is needed to tackle this problem, MSWM receives only 30-50 per cent of municipalities' budget of which only 20-50 per cent is allocated for treatment of MSW as maximum amount is spent on collection and transportation of MSW (Ghatak, 2016).

Developing countries' municipal authorities have often posed a great threat to the society and environment due to their negligent nature towards the current challenges of MSWM (Singh et al., 2014; Zurbrugg, 2003). Under these circumstances, MSWM appears difficult to envisage in the modern urban cities of developing nations like China, India, and Nepal. World Bank (2013), defines developing countries on the basis of their per capita Gross National Income (GNI) per year. Countries having GNI of 11,905 United States dollar (US$) or less are called developing countries. These countries are further subdivided as low income countries with GNI US$1,035 or less; lower middle income countries with GNI $1,036 to $4,085; upper middle income countries with GNI $4,086 to $12,615; and high income countries with GNI $12,616 or more (World Bank, 2013).

The main aim here is to better comprehend the situation of MSW in developing countries. For this purpose, one country from each of the various categories of developing countries have been selected. Such as China, which is categorised as upper middle income country and is the most populated country in the world; India which falls under lower middle income countries and is the second most populated country in the world; and Nepal is chosen from the group of low income countries. India, for example, is an agriculture-based developing country with a population of about 1.21 billion from which 377 million people live in cities (Kaushal et al., 2012). In 1994, at Surat, a city in the state of Gujarat,

India, an epidemic of plague was due to the breeding of rats over uncollected MSW blocking the drainage and water supply system (Wilson, 2007; Gupta, 2010). The people of Surat sought serious attention against the local municipal authorities (Gupta, 2010). Hence, the Indian Supreme Court decided to pass rule book to all municipal authorities and pollution control boards. The draft of the *Municipal Solid Wastes (Management and Handling) Rules*, 2000 and recently *Solid Wastes Management Rules*, 2016 was proposed in the notification of the Government of India in the MoEFCC (MoEF, 2000; MoEFCC, 2016). Still after the formation of these rule books about 90 per cent of MSW in India is disposed off unscientifically in open dumps and landfills, creating problems to environment and public health (Sharholy et al., 2008; Ghatak, 2016). It is also assessed that lack of citizens' awareness and attitude towards MSWM create a gap between different formal and informal sectors of MSWM (Medina, 2010; Guerrero et al., 2013). To make the MSWM sustainable citizens and stakeholders' corporations need to be more responsible during waste generation and disposal, specifically for waste reduction at source.

MSW Generation

The quantity of MSW generated is mostly associated with the economic status of a society, hence regions with lower Gross Domestic Product (GDP) have lower MSW generation rate (Shekdar, 2009; Guerrero et al., 2013). Table 2 shows GDP of the selected developing countries and certain cities of India together with MSW generation rates. These rates were calculated with the help of available data from various sources provided in the separate column of the table for particular countries and cities. In addition, it also explains that the higher GDP per capita resulted in higher MSW generation rate between developing countries like China, India and Nepal. The same pattern has been found between the Indian cities like Delhi and Patna. In India, two specific cities Delhi and Patna were chosen for detailed analysis of MSW generation rates. Though these cities share certain similarities particularly in factors related to MSW generation, such as increasing pace of urbanisation, high

Table 2: MSW generation rate in selected developing nations and few Indian cities

Developing Countries		GDP per capita (in current US$)	Year of study	MSW Generation (kg/capita/ day)	Source
China		4,433.3	2010	1.1	World Bank Group, 2010; Tian et al., 2013
India		1,509.2	2011	0.34	World Bank Group, 2011; Srivastava et al., 2014
Nepal		699.1	2012	0.317	World Bank Group, 2012; Saito, 2013
Specific cities of India	Delhi	2323.45	2010-11	0.367	ESR 2013; CPCB, 2015; Census of India, 2011
	Patna	590.01	2010-11	0.037	ESR 2011; CPCB, 2015; Census of India, 2011

Source: Developed by different sources provided in separate column for each row.

rate of population growth mainly due to migration yet there are drastic differences between these cities (Raj and Singh, 2017). Delhi being the national capital of the country has better infrastructure to handle the MSW while Patna is the capital of one of the most underdeveloped states in India, Bihar and has been declared as the "Garbage city" by the High Court (Raj and Raj, 2015). Hence, Patna is less equipped to deal with the rising volume of MSW. This type of MSW volume variation and generation data is helpful to sketch the most appropriate collection and disposal system (Kaushal et al., 2012).

While China generated 148.4 million tonne of MSW in 2006, its urban population alone generated 268.92 million tonne of MSW in 2010. This shows that rapid growth in the economy and growing population have a direct influence on the increasing amount of MSW (Chen, et al., 2010; Tian et al., 2013). The total MSW generated is estimated about 1435 or 52400 tonnes by 58 municipalities of Nepal. In Nepal, household wastes contribute, about 50-75 per cent of the total MSW produced (Saito, 2013). While in India 2009-12 study conducted by Central Pollution Control Board (CPCB), evaluated that 46.5 million tonne MSW was generated per year. Most of the Indian cities show an eight-fold increase in MSW since 1947 with a rate of increase 1-1.33 per cent per capita MSW per year (Kaushal et al., 2012). Some of the major cities in India, such as Delhi generated approximately 2.48–2.92 million tonne of MSW per year till 2010-11 (Mandal et al., 2014; CPCB, 2015). The quantity of MSW generated in Patna ranges from 0.08237- 0.292 million tonne MSW per year in the 2011 (Bhanu et al., 2014; CPCB, 2015).

MSW Composition

Not only wealth, but also lifestyle alteration enhances consumer behavioural changes which significantly influence MSW composition (Zurbrugg, 2003). The MSW composition can vary considerably between countries and even cities having different cultures, climatic conditions, livelihood, lifestyle practices, and dietary habits (Raj and Raj, 2015). Some examples are illustrated in Figure 1.

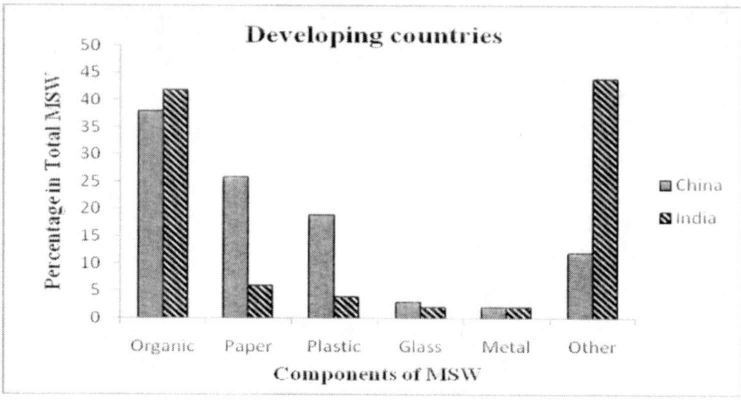

Figure 1: MSW composition of selected developing countries China, India during 2009-12.

Source: Hoornweg and Bhada-Tata, 2012.

Increasing income accelerates utilisation of fast food, processed and packaged food due to which amount of recyclable, specifically waste paper and plastics have increased while organic wastes have decreased in the MSW stream as noticed in China (Chen et al., 2010). From Figure 1, it is apparent that the amount of organic waste is more in India compared to China. This might be attributed to the differential food habits prevalent in India and China. To illustrate, in India a large proportion of the MSW is generated from households of which a considerable proportion is kitchen waste comprising of vegetables' peels, cooked and leftover food items, etc. these are organic in nature (Raj and Raj, 2015; Raj and Raj, 2018). On the other hand, in China, due to more urbanised lifestyle and easy accessibility of packaged food, the nature of kitchen waste and hence MSW changes, as there are more waste generated from packaging, such as paper, plastic, glass, etc. (*ibid*). While in Nepal almost 56 per cent of the total MSW generated is organic in nature (Saito, 2013). Hence, it can be argued that level of economic development is inversely related to the amount of organic waste production. This trend in turn influences the amount of recyclable wastes within MSW. Thus, recyclable variations can also be found between different Indian cities like Delhi and Patna due to similar factors discussed above. Such variations are illustrated in Figure 2.

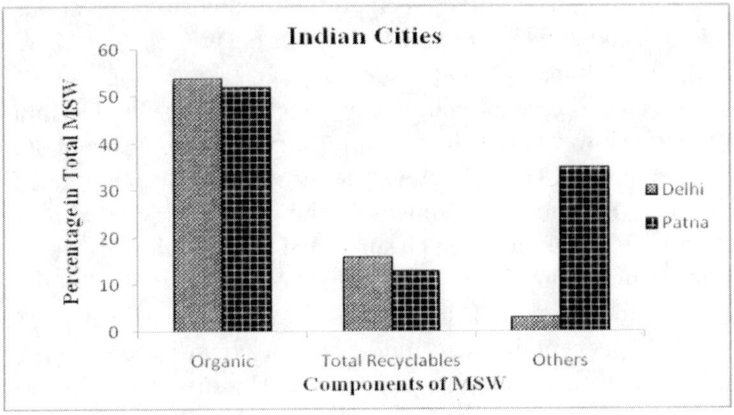

Figure 2: MSW composition of selected Indian cities.

Source: Hoornweg and Bhada-Tata, 2012.

The MSW composition can vary considerably between cities like Patna and Delhi having different cultures, climatic conditions, livelihood, lifestyle practices, and dietary habits (Raj and Raj, 2015; Raj and Raj, 2018). The organic content of MSW in both the cities of India is approximately equal though Patna has less population than Delhi. This might be due to less use of fast food, packaged and processed food in Patna. Other waste consists of textile, rubber, ash, multi laminates, appliances, e-waste, construction and demolition waste, and other inert substances. Unlike Delhi, Patna has a high quantity of waste classified as "other" (Hoornweg and Bhada-Tata, 2012). This can be explained by the fact that the real estate market is rapidly expanding in Patna leading to construction of numerous buildings for residential and commercial purposes, which in turn generates large amount of construction and demolition waste while Delhi is fully saturated in terms of real estate expansion (Raj and Singh, 2017). From the preceding discussion, it can be contended that GDP along with urbanisation, lifestyle practices, and consumer behaviour effect MSW generation and composition in different geographical locations (Raj and Raj, 2015; Raj and Singh, 2017).

MSW collection and transportation

Having discussed MSW generation and composition in various developing countries it is needed to evaluate the processes of MSW collection and transportation in these region. As mentioned in the preceding section, developing countries can be sub-divided into low income, lower middle income, upper middle income, and high income countries. The collection rate of MSW is directly related with the economic development of the country (Schubeler et al.,1996). This argument can be supported by the following facts- the low-income countries have low collection rates of around 41 per cent; while in lower middle income countries it is approximately 68 per cent; 86 per cent in upper-middle income countries; and 98 per cent in high income countries, respectively (Hoornweg and Bhada-Tata, 2012). There are various systems of MSW collection, such as backyard (house-to-house), community bins, curbside pick-up, self-delivered, contracted or delegated services (Worrell et al., 2012). MSW collection, transfer, and transport are important but expensive municipal services in most of the low income and middle-income nations (Hoornweg and Bhada-Tata, 2012). Only 30-50 per cent of municipalities' of developing countries budget goes to MSWM from which 80-90 per cent of the total budget is utilised for collection and transportation while only 20-50 per cent is left for treatment of MSW (Alagoz et al., 2008; Ghatak, 2016). Hence, the budget forms the key component in determining the economics of whole MSWM system (Alagoz et al., 2008). Developing countries facing similar economic crisis have various types of vehicles, ranging from general purpose vehicles (trucks) to highly mechanised compactors for transporting MSW from community bins (Shekdar, 2009; Tchobanoglous et al., 2014). However, the use of highly mechanised compactors is rare as compared to general loader vehicles (Shekdar, 2009).

Little improvement has been found in the MSW collection area, for instance, in China total number of MSW collection and transportation vehicles increased 1.6 times more than the last decade in 2006 (Chen et al., 2010). To avoid pollution due to uncovered MSW, covered compact vehicles have been arranged in China (Zhang et al., 2010). In Nepal, only 30 per cent household segregate the MSW and remaining 70 per cent MSW collected by municipalities are mixed MSW. Here, house-to-house collection system is followed using community bins (Pokhrel and Viraraghavan, 2005). For primary and secondary transportation, majorly three types of vehicles are employed in transportation of MSW in Nepal- rickshaws, carts, and tractors, while mainly trucks are utilised for final disposal of MSW at disposal site with the collection frequency of 62 per cent (Saito, 2013).

In India, though collection process of MSW varies yet certain uniformity is maintained. For example, household waste is generally accumulated in small container of 0.016 m^3 volume that is further transferred to the community bins with capacity of 4.5-6 m^3 (Kumar et al., 2009; Kaushal et al., 2012). Also in India, handcarts and tricycles facilitate door-to-door collection and transportation of household waste along with street sweeping (Shekdar, 2009). Community bins are placed in demarcated areas within neighbourhoods and on streets. These bins are usually made up of concrete, metal, mortars and plastic (Sharholy et al., 2008; Kaushal et al., 2012). These containers are being carried by the transportation vehicle called dumper placer to the disposal site and then returned back to its original position, specifically the metallic containers, but stationary community bins are manually emptied to the tipper truck (2.08-2.49 m^3/trip) (Sharholy et al., 2008; Shekdar, 2009; Kaushal et al., 2012).

The existing infrastructure and budget in India support some municipal authorities, such that of Delhi, to collect MSW and transport it to a landfill site on a daily basis (Srivastava et al., 2014). Conversely, in some cities like Patna collection frequency is unable to support the large volume of MSW, thus resulting in MSW piling up and rotting (Bhanu and Kumar, 2014). On an average, collection frequency of MSW in India was limited to 70-72 per cent (32.6 – 33.48 million tonne) till 2012 (Nag et al., 2005; Sharholy et al., 2008; CPCB, 2015). The transportation vehicles used for the transfer of MSW in Indian cities specifically Delhi and Patna, includes transportation by common open trucks and vehicles like bullock carts, ordinary trucks, tractor and trailers, dumper placers, tippers and compactors (Kumar et al., 2009; Kaushal et al., 2012). There are limitations of the existing transportation vehicles and collection bins used in India. To illustrate a few: street sweeping and collection systems are poorly designed; number of collection bins are inadequate; collection bins are not regularly emptied; concrete bins and metallic containers are broken or in bad condition in most of the places; scattered MSW causes choking of drains; and uncovered old vehicles with low efficiency are still in use to transport MSW (Kumar et al., 2009).

Nevertheless, Tripura, Punjab and West Bengal have exhibited some good initiatives from their local authorities regarding MSWM. In addition, few more states such as, Andhra Pradesh, Chandigarh, Delhi, Goa, Gujarat, Himachal Pradesh, Karnataka, Meghalaya, Madhya Pradesh, Maharashtra, Orissa have also shown progress in waste collection, segregation, storage and transportation. House-to-house collection and transportation need more labour, increased labour cost, small collection vehicles, and transportation cost to the community bins. So it has been observed that house-to-house collection is most critical issue in the entire management of MSW in India, resurging the need of citizens' involvement in this matter (CPCB, 2015).

MSW processing

The compression of MSW is called processing, done for reducing the volume of MSW. Three main methods used are known as: immediate compression, mechanical compression, and bio-compression (Edil et al., 1990; Kavazanjian et al., 1999; Gourc et al., 2010). Immediate compression is an increasing stress causing preliminary rapid accretion of strain. Immediate compression starts taking place since the MSW has been generated naturally (Worrell and Vesilind, 2012). Mechanical compression is a physical phenomenon, condenses the void space under stress at a particle contact. Mostly compactors are used for this process during the collection of MSW or prior to any MSW treatment (Bjarngard and Edgers, 1990; Edil et al., 1990). Bio-compression includes the biochemical reaction causing reduction in void space. It occurs during the biochemical treatment methods of the MSW like composting and Anaerobic Digestion (AD) of organic part of MSW (Singh et al., 2012; Singh et al., 2014). But, this section only includes mechanical compression processing, which has been performed by mechanical compactors during collection of MSW in developing countries like China, Nepal, and India (Shekdar, 2009; Kumar et al., 2017). Even in specific cities of India like Delhi and Patna only compactors are used during the collection of MSW (Shekdar, 2009). These mechanical compactors are not enough in numbers to process the total amount of MSW generated per day in developing countries and their cities (Hoornweg and Bhada-Tata, 2012). Specifically, in Patna the compactors came into use only after 2014.

Material recovery

On the other hand, reduction in volume of MSW can also be achieved by means of material and organic nutrient recovery. Hence, emphasis on material recovery, recycling ('urban mining') is an essential requisite, as large proportions of MSW in cities comprise of materials like metal and paper (Shekdar, 2009; Hoornweg and Bhada-Tata, 2012). In MSWM recycling is an important component through which waste material is converted into reusable material that is further processed for making fresh product(s) (Sincero and Sincero, 1996). Recycling method can be adopted for various types of wastes such as plastic, glass, paper, metal, battery, organic, and electronic products. There are different issues related to the processes of recycling (Sincero and Sincero, 1996; Hoornweg and Bhada-Tata, 2012). This problem can be broadly classified as environmental, technological, economic, legislative and social (Anghinolfi et al, 2013). Recycling requires highly technical instrumentation or machines they must be made in such a manner so to avoid any kind of environmental degradation. Nevertheless, disc screens, trommel screens, conveyor system, magnetic separators, optical sorters etc., these types of equipments are very costly and hence not supported by the economy of developing countries (Worrell and Vesilind, 2012). Also recycling requires public awareness in the direction of material recovery at source to recover maximum amount of material from MSW. This can be helped by the implementation of certain laws on MSW producers and amendment in existing rules (Wilson et al., 2006; Anghinolfi et al, 2013).

From available literature, it can be gleaned that material recovery from MSW is considered as one of the options to manage natural resources. Moreover, it is also energy efficient to produce new product(s) from secondary material through recycling than virgin material (Hoornweg and Bhada-Tata, 2012). In developing countries, the informal sector has been involved at all levels of recycling and recovery of materials from MSW (Zurbrugg, 2003). Due to this practice the recovery rate varies from 5-40 per cent when average MSW generation rate is 0.77 kg/capita/day (Zurbrugg, 2003; Hoornweg and Bhada-Tata, 2012). The MSW streams of developing nations consisted of 0–70 per cent recyclable and 17–80 per cent organics (Troschinetz et al., 2009). For example, in China it had been estimated that recyclable wastes accounted for 8–10 per cent of the total amount of MSW on an average with annual rate of increase of 7.1 per cent between 1976 and 2006 (Chen et al., 2010). This increasing rate of recyclables, specifically paper and plastics, confirm the constant decrease in organic wastes of MSW stream. The recyclables consist of different materials with varying recovery rate (Sharholy et al., 2008). Some examples are iron and steel (85%), non-ferrous metals (80%), plastics (25%), rubber (47%), paper (20%), glass (13%) (Sharholy et al., 2008; Chen et al., 2010). The volume of these recyclables reaches almost 50 million tonne having a value of 8.0126 billion US$. It can be expected that material recovery and recycling industry will grow at a rapid rate in near future around the globe as studies (Shekdar, 2009; Chen et al., 2010; Zhang et al., 2010) suggest that, 400000 automobiles have been recycled in China.

Nepal, on the other hand, has approximately 29 per cent material recovery of which majorly 5-51 per cent consists of metal, paper, glass, plastic, rubber and leather (Saito, 2013). In Nepal, though no formal system is involved in reuse and recycling, it is remarkable to notice that common people recover recyclable materials at their houses and sell them to the formal or informal sectors (Pokhrel and Viraraghavan, 2005; Saito, 2013).

In India recyclables varies from 13-20 per cent. There is good performance in material recovery and recycling in India (Kumar et al., 2017). For example, maximum recovery of plastic waste is 40–80 per cent whereas the figures for developed world are only 10–15 per cent (Agarwal et al., 2005). In 1991 there was remarkable recovery of paper (14%), which was 37 per cent higher than the global paper recovery rate (Sharholy et al., 2008; Shekdar, 2009). According to CPCB (2015), Delhi has recycled about 10-12 per cent of MSW by the help of informal sector such as ragpickers and recyclable dealers (Talyan et al., 2008). Same condition of recycling is found in Patna, NGOs, ragpickers and recyclable dealers are involved in recycling business to make 10-15 per cent recovery of material (Bhanu and Kumar, 2014).

Organic nutrients recovery

Composting will be more feasible and only method in terms of organic nutrient recovery, lower operation cost, decrease water pollution, lessened environmental pollution and beneficial use of end product called compost (Taiwo et al., 2011; Jha et al., 2011). Composting is a method of converting organic waste of MSW into manure in presence of air. It can be aerobic composting and vermi-composting (Tchobanoglous et al., 1993). Aerobic composting enhances the aerobic decomposition by various methods such as passive windrow aerobic composting produces the compost by natural aeration of windrows in long period, whereas in turned windrow composting windrows are mechanically aerated (Worrell and Vesilind, 2012). Aerated static pile composting aeration is provided by air duct below the piles, whereas the in-vessel composting is performed in the designed container having high aeration control and optimum conditions (Tchobanoglous et al., 2014). Earthworms are used for composting called vermicomposting but the operating cost of these methods become so high that developing nations cannot afford them (HPSFG et al., 1996).

These above mentioned points can be illustrated with vermicomposting method. Vermicomposting apart from high operating cost can be operated only on small scale due to the use of higher level of organism i.e., earthworm (HPSFG et al., 1996;

Gajalaskhmi and Abbasi, 2004). Earthworms are very sensitive to extreme temperature variation (7°C-30°C), susceptible to sensitive foods (like citrus food), salts and toxics, they are also predator, so many-a-time they are eaten by birds (Gajalaskhmi and Abbasi, 2004). Moreover, these earthworms are very expensive, for example, while normal earthworms cost 1.54 $/kg these earthworms cost 7.87 $/kg in India. Vermicomposting is not ideal in developing countries like China, India, and Nepal due to the existing climatic conditions. The mean temperature of these developing countries shows strong variation in a year (10°C winters and 32°C summers). This temperature variation may not be suitable for the earthworm growth (Attri et al., 2010). Also high content of various toxic substances, sensitive foods, and salts in the composition of MSW in China, India, and Nepal prohibits earthworms' growth and they naturally die without composting the MSW (Gajalaskhmi and Abbasi, 2004; Attri et al., 2010). During 2010, China decomposed only 1.8 per cent of total MSW produced (Hoornweg and Bhada-Tata, 2012). Whereas, Nepal have about 70 per cent of organic waste only very few municipal cooperation is using composting for organic nutrient recovery (Pokhrel and Viraraghavan, 2005). India compost only 5-7 per cent of total MSW, at present out of 369 composting plants only 177 aerobic composting plants are operating in various states like Maharashtra (16), Goa (73), Lakshadweep (25) and Tamil Nadu (10), and more 192 are in planning stage (Handa et al., 2013; Dong et al., 2014; Mandal et al., 2014). Since 2001, Delhi has an active Bhalaswa Aerobic Composting Plant. During 2006-07 it was used to compost 135 tonne of MSW per day (MCD, 2015). But, Patna Municipal Corporation is unable to run aerobic composting plant (Pandey, 2014). Despite so many composting plants being operational the amount of MSW being decomposed is negligible. This suggests aerobic composting is not the most viable method of recycling in India with very hot and humid climatic conditions.

MSW treatment and disposal

MSW treatment and disposal is a procedure which increases the density and decreases the toxicity of MSW (Tchobanoglous et. al., 1993). It converts the conventional form of MSW into a disposable form. The methods of MSW treatment and disposal has been selected on the basis of physical and chemical properties of MSW (Rao et al., 2017). List of methods are available for MSW treatment and disposal for example open dumping, landfill, sanitary landfill (SLF), Refuse Drive Fuel (RDF), incineration, pyrolysis, and gasification (Tchobanoglous et. al., 2014; MoEFCC, 2016). Open dumping introduces the exposed areas that have been used for disposing the MSW, which remain untreated, uncovered, and not segregated (Rao et al., 2017). In contrast to open dumping, the landfill is a trench in the ground. The MSW discarded into this trench, which has been covered daily by night soil to avoid the breeding of flies and mosquitoes (Sincero and Sincero, 1996; Tchobanoglous et. al., 2014).

The landfill has a limitation of leachate seepage into the groundwater. Hence, to prevent this SLF has been preferred, because it uses the impermeable lining material (such as geotextile layer, plastic, and clay) in the bottom of a landfill (Tchobanoglous et. al., 1993; Tchobanoglous et. al., 2014). RDF treatment method has been used to produce energy from MSW, hence known as Waste-to-Energy (WTE) techniques. Under high pressure and pH, organic waste produces methane and carbon dioxide which can be used for electricity production (Singh et al., 2014). RDF is a fuel made from combustible fraction like paper, cardboard, and plastic of MSW which are further processed and pelletised. RFD can replace natural fuel like coal for the production of heat energy (Sincero and Sincero, 1996). The incineration is the combustion of MSW chemical elements in presence of oxygen at a temperature higher than 850°C resulted in ash and greenhouse gases (Young, 2010). Pyrolysis is the thermal treatment method, which degradation of carbon-containing materials of MSW at temperatures of 450 to 750°C, in the absence of oxygen to produce a carbonaceous char, oils and combustible gases (Cheremisinoff, 2003). Gasification is a thermal reaction, take place in hydrocarbons in the partial supply of oxygen to produce carbon dioxide and water at high temperature, specifically 700-1600°C (Klein and Nickolas, 2003).

The cost and feasibility of MSW treatment technologies with MSW composition as well as local conditions directly affect the treatment and disposal method options for MSW (Hoornweg and Bhada-Tata, 2012; Worrell and Vesilind, 2012; Tchobanoglous et al., 2014). Some treatment and disposal methods operating on the MSW of developing world are shown in the table 3. As evident from Table 3, maximum MSW has been openly dumped in the dumping grounds. Landfill is the second largest method used for the treatment of MSW, followed by composting recycling, incineration, and others.

Table 3: Treatment and final disposal methods of MSW in developing countries

Disposal/treatment methods	Range of MSW (million tonne)
Dumping	0.47 – 44.0
Landfill	02.2 – 80.0
Composting	0.05 – 1.30
Recycling	0.02 – 1.90
Incineration	0.05 – 0.18
Others	0.97 – 8.40

Source: Hoornweg and Bhada-Tata, 2012.

In China, safe disposal rates have been below 55 per cent since 2002 (Chen et al., 2010; Dong et al., 2014). China in 2006 had 324 MSW landfill sites which received 81.4 per cent of MSW and the proportion had diminished to 79.4 per cent in 2010 for safe disposal. Inspite of the large proportion of organic waste in MSW, composting has been diminished and incineration became more pronounced due to production of electrical energy at 0.04 US$ per kilowatt/hour for 15 years with other renewable energy resource (Chen et al., 2010; Zhang et al., 2010; Dong et al., 2014). Additionally, bottom ash generated by the incineration of MSW might substitute 1-2 per cent primary resource gravel in road and building construction so to preserve the resource, i.e., gavel (Chen et al., 2010; Dong et al., 2014; Brunner et al., 2015). In case of Nepal open dumping, including riverside and roadside dumping is practiced by 45 of the

58 municipalities and merely 37 per cent of the total MSW disposed off at SLF (Saito, 2013). Only six municipalities Kathmandu Metropolitan City (KMC), Lalitpur, Pokhara, Ghorahi, Dhankuta, and Tansen have constructed SLF sites (Pokhrel and Viraraghavan, 2005). While many municipalities have started to plan for an engineered landfill site, 14 municipalities still have no such plan (Pokhrel and Viraraghavan, 2005; Saito, 2013).

In India, MSW treatment and disposal covered only 12.45 per cent (5.79 million tonne/year) of MSW in 2012 as adapted in 39 per cent of cities such as Delhi, Mumbai, Pune, Chennai, Ahmadabad, Hyderabad, Goa, and Bangalore (Mandal et al., 2014; CPCB, 2015). The MoEFCC, Government of India had issued the *Solid Waste Management Rules*, 2016 which recommended to adopt different treatment technologies including, gasification, pyrolysis, plasma gasification, RDF, WTE combustion, and SLF (MoEFCC, 2016). Presently more than 90 per cent of MSW in cities and towns of India are directly disposed off as open dumping in the low lying land areas due to non-existence of SLF and unsuccessful treatment method (Sharholy et al., 2008; Pandyaswargo et al., 2012). The MSW composition in India is not suitable for WTE project because of its high moisture, around 50 per cent and inorganic content about 30 per cent, which results in low energy value of 3,350–4,200 kJ kg^{-1} (Chattopadhyay et al., 2009). Various WTE plants set in different regions of India remain unsuccessful for these reasons. Some examples are, large-scale AD plants in Vijaywada (20 tonne/day), and Koyambedu flower market (30 tonne/day) closed just a few months after opening due to mismatch between quality of MSW inputs and technology design (Pandyaswargo et al., 2012). The RDF plants in Deonar, Mumbai (80 tonne/day), Bangalore (5 tonne/day), Chandigarh (500 tonne/day), Hyderabad (700 tonne/day) and Vijaywada (600 tonne/day) shutdown due to low calorific value of the product from the expected calorific value (Kalyani, 2003; Pandyaswargo et al., 2012; Kalyani and Pandey, 2014). The Timarpur incineration plant in Delhi (300 tonne/day of MSW to generate 3.7 Megawatt of electric power) closed after 21 days because of low calorific value (550–850 kcal/kg whereas minimum calorific value should fall between 1200 and 1400 kcal/kg) and high organic content of MSW (Lal, 1996). There are two "on trial" incineration plants in Delhi-Ghazipur and Okhla incineration plants with capacity of 1,950 tonne/day and 1,300 tonne/day. Ghazipur incineration plant started working in June 2015 (MCD, 2015). Okhla incineration plant established by Jindal Urban Infrastructure Limited started operating successfully in 2012, generating 16 MW of electricity from 1350 tonne/day MSW (ibid). In addition, a gasification unit started in New Delhi in Gual Pahari (Pandyaswargo et al., 2012; Kalyani and Pandey, 2014).

In Delhi, 75 per cent of MSW is dumped into open landfill sites. Only 5-7 per cent of MSW is composted, as already mentioned in the recycling and recovery section, yet approximately 20 per cent of MSW remain unattended in open areas posing health hazards and causing ecological imbalances to land, water and air (Ahsan, 1999; Ambulkar and Shekdar, 2004; Mandal et al., 2014). Since 1975, around 20 such landfills have been created in Delhi, 15 of which have already been exhausted and two have been found unfit and suspended (Ahsan, 1999; Ambulkar and Shekdar, 2004). At present, three landfill sites in Delhi are operational, namely Gazipur, Bhalswa, and Okhla which are devoid of LFG (Landfill Gas); leachate collection; and treatment system (Ambulkar and Shekdar, 2004). Talyan et al., (2008) estimate that these landfills contribute to about 80 per cent of the total methane emission in Delhi. Deposited MSW at these landfills can yield an average of 95 m^3 CH_4/tonnes, having a calorific value of 19.43 MJ/m^3. Assuming a conversion efficiency of 25 per cent and overall generator efficiency of 80 per cent, electrical energy can be produced from LFG at a rate of 12.98×10^5 kWh/year (Ambulkar and Shekdar, 2004; Talyan et al., 2008). However, MCD (Municipal Corporation of Delhi) has not yet considered these consequences which will cause great harm to environment and a loss of a potential source of energy (MCD, 2015).

Conversely, in Patna since 2010 about 65 per cent of the total waste has been attended and the remaining unattended 35 per cent MSW are still strewn beside roads, parks, playgrounds and vacant land (UD and HD, 2010). At present in Patna, MSW does not have any proper disposal/treatment method but open dumping of MSW in low-lying areas as well as at the outskirts of the city besides the existing dumping ground is in practice (Bhanu et al., 2014). Such unscientific practices cause immense air and ground water pollution. It was evident from a study conducted about ambient air quality and ground water for a range of physiochemical parameters that were beyond the permissible limit at two dumping sites in Patna (Kumari et al., 2011).

In Patna the dumping ground is situated at Ilahibagh, Ramachak-Bairiya village with the land areas of approximately 74 acres. Patna has reserved it for development of WTE plant including sanitary landfill (BUIDC, UD and HD, 2014). The landfill site at Bairiya is surrounded by six densely populated villages whose total population is estimated to be around 20,000. The habitants are facing environmental problems and chronic health issues such as respiratory tract inflammation, permanent respiratory problems as smoke produced due to unsafe burning of MSW being dumped since 2010 consist of high amount of pollutants (Bhanu et al., 2014). The villagers have filed a petition against the Bairiya landfill site in Patna High Court in November 2012. As per the Master Plan of Patna 2031, Ramchak Bairiya area has again been suggested as a sanitary landfill and WTE plant site. Despite the fact that it is surrounded by the habitation and not adhering to the *Municipal Solid Wastes (Management and Handling) Rules*, 2000. Nevertheless, Patna Municipal Corporation (PMC) considers it as a waste mismanagement and misunderstanding of MSWM project (Bhanu et al., 2014).

Stakeholders and public awareness

At the onset of this section it is pertinent to describe what we understand by stakeholders. Based on our understanding of the issues and challenges of MSW we contend that in respect to MSWM every individual should be considered to be a stakeholder as all of us are responsible for production of waste hence we all should take the onus for its effective management. However, some formal definitions of stakeholders have been provided by certain scholars and we shall groom our discussion around these definitions. Joseph et al., (2006) define stakeholders as group of people and organisations interested in MSW management, and participating in activities that make it achievable. According to Guerrero et al., (2013) formal stakeholder includes central government ministries, local and central municipal authorities as most of the policies and provisions of MSWM are structured by them. Private contractors, public, NGOs are also important MSWM stakeholders, as opined by certain scholars (Joseph et al., 2006; Guerrero et al., 2013). However, they contend that education and research institutions, funding agencies, political parties and media are less mentioned in formal sector as stakeholders of MSWM. Guerrero et al. (2013), state that informal stakeholders include nomadic MSW buyers, ragpickers, junk shop owners, and street sweepers. Studies have emphasised that MSWM assessment has less consideration for social aspects (Halla et al., 1999; Allesch et al., 2014).

In India, problems related to stakeholders and public awareness has also been identified (Ojok et al., 2014). It has been noted that absence of coordination and partnership among different departments of civic bodies is responsible for poor management of MSW (Srivastava et al., 2005). Apart from various social stakeholders and legal issues of MSWM, public apathy and low social status has created worst situation in developing countries (Srinivasan, 2006). Even during policy making different ongoing developmental projects and barren lands were not considered for MSWM (specifically MSW disposal and treatment) which later become residential areas (Srivastava et al., 2005; Srinivasan, 2006; Vij, 2012). Hence, serious attention is required for proper planning and new policies should be implemented to cover all the existing gaps. A new charge based on 'Polluters Pay Principle' (MSW producer is responsible for producing pollution hence they have to pay for the damage done to the natural environment) can be imposed on people for complete MSWM activities (Vij, 2012; Ojok et al., 2014). Since citizens are the producers of MSW, community involvement is mandatory for MSWM. To receive a lively public participation, governing authorities and NGOs need to take strong steps such as regular campaigns to create awareness among the peoples, and educate them to manage MSW at individual level (Srinivasan, 2006; Vij, 2012). The knowledge of public health hazards caused due to MSW and lack of MSWM can help to sensitise the community. Hence, there is a requirement of discussion related to MSWM and public health.

Hazardous impacts of MSW on health

WHO (1947:1) defines health as a "state of çomplete physical, mental, and social well-being, and not merely the absence of disease or infirmity." The perpetual adjustment and adaptation by the body to various changes inside and outside the body, for example, stress and climatic changes for the maintainance of homeostatsis is also known as health (Moeller, 2005). When question arises for the protection and prevention of community health then it can be pronounced as public health (Acheson, 1988; Moeller, 2005). A British governmental committee during the year 1988, describes public health as "the science and art of preventing disease, prolonging life and promoting health through organised community efforts" (Acheson, 1988:2). Public health is also affected by the polluted surroundings caused due to anthropogenic reasons like MSW, such a scenario has been studied under environmental health. Although environmental health is a section of public health, that involves assessing, understanding, and managing the effects of peoples on the environment and environmental impact on them (Moeller, 2005; Gutschmidt et al., 2010). Various health disorders initiated, progressed, sustained, or characterised in a healthy person, are triggered by environmental factors (Gutschmidt et al., 2010). Hence, identifying an interrelationship between life and environment is the foremost priority of public health. WHO (2019) gives definition for environmental health as,

> *Environmental health addresses all the physical, chemical, and biological factors external to a person, and all the related factors impacting behaviour. It encompasses the assessment and control of those environmental factors that can potentially affect health. It is targeted towards preventing disease and creating health-supportive environments. This definition excludes behaviour not related to environment, as well as behaviour related to the social and cultural environment, and genetics.*

Health is the highest priority for the growth of any developing country. That means public health needs a serious attention against environmental issues (WHO, 2011). Since MSW produces hazardous substances which keep on accumulating in the environment, thus increasing load of pollutants and disturbing the environmental balance which ultimately affect population health (Bogner et al., 2008). In developing countries like India, cities like Patna is facing a serious problem of MSWM. The hazardous impacts on the environment, ecology, and public health are due to different pollutants of MSW which on escalating. List of pollutants such as furans, dioxins, and microorganisms are generated through unattended MSW and on exposure to these pollutants community get infected which results in serious diseases such as Diarrhea/Dysentery, Acute Respiratory Infection (ARI), and Asthma/Chronic Respiratory Diseases (CRD) (Rushton, 2003; Koroneos and Nanaki, 2012). Due to profound occurrence of these diseases, this study has been focused on vector born disease, ARI, and CRD. Table 4 gives a snapshot of pollutants, source of MSW and health hazards. This table comprises a list of different components of MSW from which certain amount of pollutant arises, and on exposure or prolonged exposure to these pollutants can lead to health hazards. Such as, the food scraps and animal waste present in MSW allow the growth of saprophytic bacteria species like Brucella, Shigella, Yersinia etc.

Table 4: Hazardous impact of MSW originated pollutants to the human health on exposure

Pollutants	Source of pollutant in MSW	Health hazards
Saprophytic bacteria some species: Brucella, Campylobacter, Listeria, Salmonella, Shigella, Yersinia	Food scraps and animal waste	Serious infections, brucellosis, campylobacteriosis, listeriosis, salmonellosis, shigellosis, and yersiniosis.
Gram-negative bacteria	Organic waste	Acute systemic disorder, respiratory symptoms, acute lung function changes. Chronic effect of endotoxin exposure: chronic obstructive pulmonary disease
Heavy Metals: Arsenic (Ar)	Wood preservatives, paints, dyes, and semiconductors. May release during the burning of waste.	Injurious impact on skin, mucous membranes and the nervous system. Repeated and prolong exposure: damage to skin and the peripheral blood vessels
Viruses: like, hepatitis, HIV and hemorrhagic viruses and prions	Special case, when biomedical waste is present in MSW.	Hepatitis, HIV, hemorrhagic fever
Volatile organic compounds (VOCs) such as; benzene, toluene, dichloromethane, tetrachloroethylene, trichloroethylene, phthalates, and dime-thylacetamide	Metabolic activity of microorganisms on organic waste	Eyes and respiratory tract infection. VOCs are carcinogenic, mutagenic.
Dioxins, furans and polyaromatic hydrocarbon (PAH)	Plastic (PVC, PCBs etc.)	Damaging the immunity and nervous system, reproductive functions, allergic dermatitis, chloracne and gastrointestinal disturbances, anemia and liver damage. Reported carcinogenic in nature.

Sources: Schwartz et al., 1993; Seaton et al., 1995; Romieu et al., 2002; Douwes et al., 2003; Diaz et al., 2005; Bunger et al., 2007; Meeker et al., 2009; Kone et al., 2012; Koroneos and Nanaki, 2012; Laitinen et al., 2016

When community come across the dumping ground or road side strewed with MSW, these bacteria enter into their bodies through air passage. This results in the bacterial infections called brucellosis, shigellosis, and yersiniosis (Douwes et al., 2003; Diaz et al., 2005; Bunger et al., 2007). It is important to note that the diversity of MSW gives rise to diverse pollutants, from different sources that have health consequences.

MSWM and public health

Around the globe, MSWM is regarded as highly needed and arduous task. For that reason, MSWM procedure must include factors like public health and safety, economy, environmental protection, and sustainability (Sharholy et al., 2008). Lack of MSWM leads to an increase in pollutants that pollute air, water, and soil resulting into perilous effects on public health (Shekdar, 2009). In the nineteenth century, epidemics such as cholera used to spread due to pathogenically contaminated water (Giusti, 2009). Also epidemics like plague occurred because of poor MSW management in developing countries such as India (Gupta, 2010). Developing countries are also well known for the direct health effects caused by unsafe MSWM (Cointreau-Levine, 1997). Development in scientific treatment and disposal methods of MSWM, may serve as an answer to the exponentially increasing amount of MSW with better organisation. The changing lifestyle has been followed by physiognomies of MSW which resulted in huge accumulation of new pollutants such as dioxins in MSW stream (Giusti, 2009; Raj and Raj, 2015). Prolonged health hazards of exposure to such chemical compounds found in MSW or formed during MSW treatment and disposal are hard to quantify. Specifically, when they are present in very less amount and when different exposure routes are available like food and land contamination. Many studies (Rushton, 2003; Alam and Ahmade, 2013; WHO, 2016) have recognised the health effects of MSW worldwide.

A list of development has been reported with time such as innovative MSWM technologies, strengthened legislative rules, and advanced health facilities. But still, the assurance for any MSW treatment center or disposal facilities has remained questionable for the community (Hoornweg and Bhada-Tata, 2012). Every progressive move of MSW and its management has been related to harmful health problems. This association of MSW and health effects can be direct or indirect (Rushton, 2003; Alam and Ahmade, 2013). Direct health impacts are associated with MSW handling; recovery of materials; treatment methods such as incinerators and landfills exposure; and recycling (Englehardt et al., 2000). Whereas, indirect health effects occur due to the import of pollutants produced from MSW to contaminate the atmosphere, land, water, and edibles (Englehardt et al., 2000; Giusti, 2009). Hence, according to the existing information regarding the health hazards of MSW, this section has been divided into three sub-sections: studies conducted on health hazards of MSW; youth and indirect health effects of MSW; health hazards due to lack of MSWM. Consequently, further studies can be structured to reduce the health hazards, improvise health safety and encourage a sustainable solution.

Studies conducted on health hazards of MSW

Health hazards found in ragpickers and sanitary workers are more pronounced due to the direct contact with MSW. The ragpickers exhibited a higher prevalence of low haemoglobin, high circulating eosinophil and monocyte counts, unhealthy gums, frequent diarrhoea, and dermatitis when compared to controls (Ray et al., 2004). Their sputum showed an abundance of alveolar macrophages, siderophages, and inflammatory cells, and a very high frequency of squamous metaplasia and dysplasia of bronchial epithelial cells, suggesting inflammation and cellular changes in the airways (Ray et al., 2004; da Silva et al., 2006). Health effects on the peoples living in the vicinity of the landfill/incinerator plants of MSW has also been reported. A study by Elliott et al., (2001) suggests small risks of congenital anomalies and low and very low birth weight in the population living near landfill sites. Similarly, people living around the MSW incineration plant, the rate of congenital anomalies was not significantly higher in exposed communities as compared to unexposed communities. Among exposed communities trend of risk with increasing exposure was observed for obstructive uropathies (Cordier et al., 2004).

Indirect health hazards of MSW on population are due to various pollutants in the proximate atmosphere. The effect of MSW pollutants on health can be studied in terms of mixed pollutants from all sources. Such as Delhi has an increasing level of air pollution, due to which people suffer from respiratory diseases that may lead to death sometimes. Similar results were also found for water pollution. The contaminated water can be groundwater or surface water (Cointreau-Levine, 1997; Englehardt et al., 2000; Chatterjee, 2001; Giusti, 2009; Tian et al., 2013). The indirect effects of MSW on human health require intense research. Specifically, the most exposed fraction of the human population i.e., youth. Youth have more frequent exposure to MSW pollutants due to an active lifestyle. Correspondingly, prolonged indirect exposure will enhance the amount and rate of pollutant entrance in the body. Hence, the relationship among indirect health effects of MSW and youth is essential to be understood.

Youth and indirect health effects of MSW

The term youth is defined as population in age group between 10 and 24 years (WHO, 1999). United Nation explains that the young generation belong to the age group of 15 and 24 years (UN Secretariat, 1981). In India "Youth are defined as women and men falling in the age group of 15-24 years" (Parasuraman et al., 2009: ii). The definition of young people is highly influenced by surrounding factors like demographic condition, financial state, society, and cultural background. However, in this book we consider, WHO designated definition of young population who belong to the age group of 10 and 24 years.

MSW has a substantial influence on greenhouse gases CO_2, CH_4, and N_2O elevated amount of which is one of the leading causes of indirect health effects of MSW (Bogner et al., 2008; Giusti, 2009). Such an increasing level of greenhouse gases leads to climate change such as depletion of ozone layer which upthrusted the climatic temperature. Climate change has serious health effects in young population (Bogner et al., 2008; Alam and Ahmade, 2013). For younger population, respiratory issues become more pronounced like acute respiratory infections, and asthma (Giusti, 2009; WHO, 2016). Moreover, the incidences of vector-borne diseases, for example, malaria, typhoid, diarrhoea and dysentery diseases, become a regular phenomenon in places with poor MSWM practices (Englehardt et al., 2000; Giusti, 2009).

The key indirect mediums that transport the contamination from MSW into the human bodies are inhalation of polluted air and consuming the contaminated food and water (Giusti, 2009). Air and water have been polluted due to the presence of particulate matters, ash, dust, methane, carbon dioxide, nitrous oxide, hydrogen sulphide, bio-aerosols, heavy metals, dioxins, and pathogens etc. (Englehardt et al., 2000; Saffron et al., 2003; Giusti, 2009). These pollutants arise from MSW and its different handling methods for instance land spread, open burning, open dumping, landfills, incineration, composting and recycling (Giusti, 2009; Goorah et al., 2009; Alam and Ahmade, 2013).

The exposure to emitted pollutants can be direct or indirect. The MSW handlers and the population living in the vicinity of MSW treatment process face the health hazards due to its direct exposure. MSW emitted pollutant follow indirect pathway via contaminating breathing air, available water sources and soil used for fertilisation. This contamination passes to food chain by polluted water and soil, whereas air pollution enters during inhalation by the communities. Such indirect exposure leads to community health hazards; young population suffer from respiratory disorders while old people experience cardiovascular disorders.

Climatic changes also lead to destruction of environmental condition. For example, expanding sea level, utmost weather conditions and unusual floods. The reason behind all calamities is global warming, triggered by the increasing greenhouse gases (Bogner et al., 2008). MSW and MSWM technologies have a significant role in enhancing the amount of CO_2 (carbon dioxide),

CH_4 (methane), Volatile Organic Compounds (VOCs) and N_2O (nitrous oxide) in the atmosphere (Goldberg, 1995; Smith et al., 2001; Bogner et al., 2008). The piled up MSW develop the anaerobic condition in open dumping grounds and landfills leading to AD of organic waste (Goldberg, 1995). This biodegradation generates biogas, which emits higher concentration of VOCs, sulphur containing compound, CH_4, CO_2 with a considerable amount of N_2O (Goldberg, 1995; Singh et al., 2012; Singh et al., 2014).

Smith et al., (2001) refer to European Union-15 (EU-15) atmospheric emission of greenhouse gases with the percentage contribution of MSW during 1994. In reports that the CO_2 emitted during the year 1994 was 3215 Mt; having one global warming potential (over 100 years) from which less than 0.5 percent had been contributed by MSW respectively (Smith et al., 2001; Bogner et al., 2008). Correspondingly, CH_4 and N_2O overall emission in 1994 was 22 Mt and 1.05 Mt respectively, in which MSW contribution percentage was 33 and 01 respectively. Both CH_4 and N_2O also possess global warming potential (over 100 years) was 21 and 310 respectively (Smith et al., 2001; Bogner et al., 2008; Giusti, 2009). These outcomes prove that the emerging pollutants from MSW into the environment are deteriorating the health of the community specifically youth, and expose them to high health risks.

The effect of MSW and MSWM processes on public health can be examined precisely through epidemiological analysis. The epidemiological study performs an essential investigation regarding the relationship of MSW pollutant and its exposure for a specific health hazard. The relationship is generally computed in terms of ratio known as Relative Risk (RR) (Saffron et al., 2003; Viera, 2008). The RR is a proportion of exposed population disease incidence cases to the unexposed population of same disease incidence cases (Saffron et al., 2003; Giusti, 2009). Whereas, Odd Risk (OR) is specifically used in the case-control analysis, which is the proportion of the odds of the disease incidence in the exposed group to the odds of the disease incidence in the control group (Viera, 2008). A particular health hazard spread resulted in an increased risk that would be denoted by relative risk greater than one (RR>1). The greater value of RR is statistically significant confirmation of the hazardous impact on public health due to serious environmental elements (Tomatis, 1990). Then again, owing to the devastating huge epidemiological investigation on MSW management relationship with health issues, the odds ratio or relative risk have been reported less than 1.5 but in few cases, it has been found more than two (Tomatis, 1990; Saffron et al., 2003; Giusti, 2009).

The two RR can be pronounced as doubling of health risk due to MSW, but if RR equals to 1.1 it can be called 10 per cent increase in the risk (Tomatis, 1990; Saffron et al., 2003). Though a relationship of MSW and health issues is strong but statistically not significant, then it cannot be considered for further studies of interconnection (Saffron et al., 2003; Giusti, 2009). This explains indirect pathways followed by MSW pollutants and risk they cause to human health. It also shows that public health is directly proportional to the increasing amount of MSW. However, lack of evidence regarding health effect specifically on youth, encourages further study on indirect health hazardous that has been pronounced in the young population.

Health hazards due to lack of MSWM

As evident from the previous sections, cities like Patna face serious problem of MSWM. The MSW pollutants are the cause of health hazards, while potential of pollutants can be evaluated by the analysis of some important factors such as mobility, toxicity, bioaccumulation, environmental persistence and other hazards like flammable (Alam and Ahmade, 2013; Rushton, 2003). On the basis of these factors, ten pollutants which have been listed highest in causing potential health hazards include cadmium, mercury, arsenic, chromium, nickel, dioxins, polychlorinated biphenyls (PCB), polycyclic aromatic hydrocarbon (PAH), particulate matter (PM10), and sulphur dioxide (SO_2) (Floret et al., 2003; Rushton, 2003; MoEFCC, 2016; Pivnenko et al., 2016). Various studies such as Elliott et al., (2001), Ray et al., (2004), Cordier et al., (2004), and da Silva et al., (2006) have been conducted on ragpickers, sanitary workers, people living around landfills and incinerators revealing the serious health hazards of MSW. Some of these are the very high frequency of squamous metaplasia, dysplasia of bronchial epithelial cells, risks of congenital anomalies, cardiac anomalies, obstructive uropathies and skin anomalies (Elliott et al., 2001; Ray et al., 2004; Cordier et al., 2004; Tian et al., 2013).

Though we can discuss in details the list of pollutants; source of pollutant in MSW and MSWM, and health hazards, but in this book we will restrict to few examples for better understanding. For example, food scraps and animal waste found in MSW decomposes to produce saprophytic bacteria, that on exposure can cause bacterial infection like brucellosis, camphylobacteriosis, shigellosis, listeriosis, salmonellosis and yersiniosis. Organic waste also produces fungi, gram negative and gram positive bacteria bioaerosols which is responsible for infectious mycosis, acute systemic respiratory symptoms, allergic alveolitis, anthrax and tetanus. Prolonged exposure to endotoxins can even cause chronic obstructive pulmonary disease. A special case of viruses can be found in MSW, if biomedical waste has been thrown in MSW community bins. These viruses can spread HIV, hepatitis and hemorrhagic fever. Apart for air pollution transmission of bacteria and fungi to human body vectors such as flies and mosquitoes can transfer pathogenic bacteria and parasitic worms inside the houses which cause different diseases like Q fever, leptospirosis, amebiasis, and toxoplasmosis etc. Along with organic waste MSW also consists of wood, paints, dyes, plastic, steel, lead, glass, ceramic, computer screens, fluorescent lights, textile, rubber etc. These all components of MSW also degrade and release different heavy metals, for example, arsenic, cadmium, lead, mercury, and chromium. These metals on exposure can lead to skin infection, respiratory tract infection, blood vessel rupture, nervous system infection, and pneumonitis in human bodies. Whereas prolonged infection can even cause skin, peripheral blood vessel, kidney and liver damage; cancer; infertility and fetus damage. MSWM process such as composting, landfill, and incineration produces gases such as ammonia (NH_3), nitric oxide (NO), nitrogen dioxide (NO_2),

N_2O, sulphur dioxide (SO_2), hydrogen sulphide (H_2S), methyl mercaptan (CH_4S), VOCs etc. Primary exposure can cause eye, skin, and respiratory irritation, but prolonged expose can cause serious diseases like cancer, lung oedema, pulmonary tissue damage, asthmatic attack, fertility effects, cardiovascular system effects and weaken the immune system etc.

MSW pollutants have followed the indirect pathways like food chain contamination and air pollution. Hence the pollutants quickly enter the human body through contaminated food, water, and air. Therefore, the general population has been suffering from health hazardous specifically, its sub-group i.e., young population. Youth are more likely to suffer from respiratory diseases and vector-borne diseases due to MSW pollutant exposure. Furthermore, to avoid such health risks a preventive MSWM model is needed to be developed for developing countries. The ISSWM concept has provided that opportunity.

Integrated sustainable solid waste management

MSWM is not limited within the boundaries of technological system facilitating handling and disposal of MSW (Wilson et al., 2013). Rather it also deals with many other factors such as, policy and legal framework; institutional arrangements; operations management; financial management; public participation and awareness; and action plan for improvement with respect to sustainability (Scheinberg et al., 2010). For sustainable MSWM it is necessary to rationalize functionality by integrating all elements that govern performance within the system (Shekdar, 2009). This process may be termed as Integrated Sustainable Solid Waste Management (ISSWM) which inspires technically applicable, economically feasible, and socially satisfactory solutions to MSWM issues and challenges (Van de Klundert et al., 2001). The ISSWM framework involves four basic principles and three major dimensions- equity (citizen participation in MSWM for healthy environment); effectiveness (Application of efficient MSWM model for safe and complete disposal of MSW); efficiency (MSWM with minimum cost, maximum benefit and appropriate resource intake under consideration of equity, effectiveness and sustainability); and sustainability (MSWM system is suitable to the local conditions and feasible for a technical, social, economic, environmental, financial, institutional and legal/political perspective) (Scheinberg, 2001; Scheinberg, 2010; Wilson et al., 2013).

Van de Klundert et al. (2001) explain that these four principles are based on three major interlinked dimensions, namely, stakeholders, MSW processing system, and different aspects of planning and management. As explained earlier, to attain sustainable MSWM these three dimensions are embedded in ISSWM sphere. Where the stakeholders dimension (includes all local authorities, NGOs/CBOs, service users, formal sectors, informal sectors, donor agencies) develop different laws, policies, models and resources to facilitate MSW processing system dimension and aspect of planning and management dimension with the help of above explained four principles. To check their suitability remaining two dimensions (MSW processing system dimension and aspect of planning and management dimension) applied laws, policies, models and resources to the current scenario of MSW for particular place or area. Sustainable MSWM only can be possible when all three dimensions are integrated with each other to continue the back and forth flow of information.

The European Union (EU) funded programme in Asia (www. issowama.net) uses ISSWM as a project specific approach to assess the typical success or failure factors of running MSWM system (Wilson et al., 2013). They suggested that, wherever, the major backlogs of MSWM have been identified, it should be dealt with to create sustainability in the integrated solid waste management system for a country or a particular area (Zurbrügg et al., 2012). Hence, the concept of ISSWM is significant for this study but few factors may be twisted according to the study area conditions i.e., climatic conditions; public behaviour and attitude; governing authorities, policies followed for MSWM; existing MSWM system; private sector contribution.

4

Waste Management to Reduce Health Hazards in Patna

The problem of solid waste management is accentuated in a city like Patna, the capital city of Bihar which is one of the most underdeveloped provinces of India. A large proportion of the solid waste in Patna is generated from households. Studies by various organisations have noted that household solid waste is one of the most difficult sources of solid waste to manage because of its diverse range of composite materials. A considerable portion of household waste consists of organic matters resulting from the preparation and consumption of food, including vegetable peelings and waste food. It also consists of plastics, paper, glass, textiles, cellophane, metals and some hazardous waste from household products such as paint, garden pesticides, pharmaceuticals, fluorescent tubes, personal care products, batteries containing heavy metals and discarded wood treated with dangerous substances such as anti-fungal and anti-termite chemicals. Improper handling, storage and disposal of wastes are major causes of environmental pollution, which provides breeding grounds for pathogenic organisms and encourages the spread of infectious diseases. The most common diseases caused by improper waste management are typhoid and paratyphoid fever, diarrhea and dysenteries, cholera, hook worm and various intestinal parasitic diseases, viral hepatitis, poliomyelitis and other viral infections. Hence, it is essential to segregate the waste at source, as it would help in the proper treatment and management of organic and inorganic wastes, thus preventing spread of diseases.

The situation of MSW and lack of MSWM has become grave because of the irresponsible behaviour of public and institutional authorities. Consequently, MSW has become a prominent source of hazards for both the human and the environment. The uncollected and mismanaged MSW which remains strewn on the roadside and housing localities many-a-time clog already wrecked drainage system in Patna. Such unsafe and inadequate management of MSW causes the spread of disease causing pathogens as bacteria, viruses, particulate matter, dioxins and other harmful pollutants in the surroundings and atmosphere (Romieu et al., 2002; Kone et al., 2012). Hence, due to the repeated exposure of these local sources of pollutants lead to serious health problems in young population, who are most mobile and more exposed to these wastes, such as Diarrhea/ Dysentery, Acute Respiratory Infection (ARI), and Asthma/Chronic Respiratory Diseases (CRD) (Schwartz et al., 1993; Seaton et al., 1995; Romieu et al., 2002; Kone et al., 2012; WHO, 2017).

There is an attitudinal problem of the community regarding waste management, as they believe that the government is responsible for it. However, case studies have shown that community involvement plays a crucial role in waste management. Therefore, it is important to create awareness among the community stakeholders about the importance, necessity and their role in waste management and how effectively it can help to reduce various health hazards. Studies on community waste management have not focused on generation and managing wastes at household level though household is the smallest unit within a community and are the first point of generating various solid wastes.

The idea for this book came up when we picked up one of the thread that defined this city. After attesting to the rich historical heritage, Patna presents itself as what the State High Court declared-the "Garbage City" of the country. Figure 3 shows a street sign in Hindi welcoming people to the city of Patna. The streets of Patna are strewn with garbage (Figures 4 and 5) which is not only displeasing sight but also have several environmental concerns.

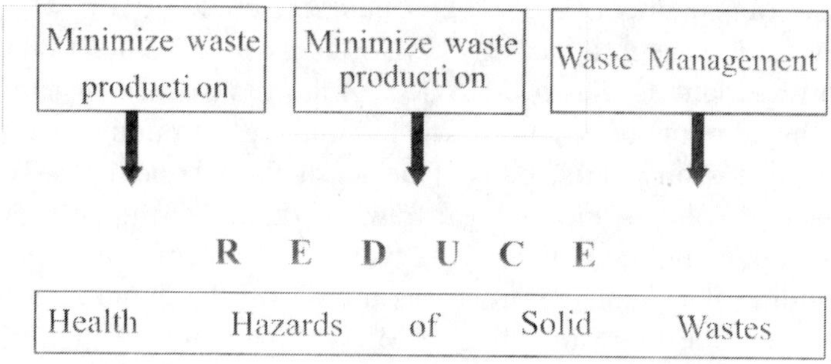

However, in this book it is not our contention to provide a detailed analysis of the project, rather we intend to draw from the major findings which would provide a case study to better comprehend the processes and practices of waste production and management in Patna.

Like other cities of developing countries, waste production in Patna is also affected by these three interconnected factors of population growth, urbanisation and increased consumption. Patna is the most populated districts in Bihar with the decadal growth rate of population (2001-2011) being 22.34 per cent, and population density of 1,102 persons per square kilometre (Census of India 2011). The increase in population growth rate in Patna is attributed to dual causes of natural increase, due to high fertility rate, as well as high rate of rural to urban migration. Patna is also the most urbanised district in Bihar, with an urbanisation rate of 43.5 per cent, much higher than the national average (*ibid*). Patna ranks very high in terms of solid waste generation in India and in Bihar (2011) 52 per cent of the waste generated is organic in nature and only 13 per cent of the total waste is recyclable. Due to lack of industries in Patna, a large proportion of the waste is generated from households, hotels, resorts, restaurants, and other businesses. The current scenario of MSWM in Patna is neither integrated nor sustainable and this situation places environment and young population health at potential risk (Kumari et al., 2011; Bhanu and Kumar, 2014).

An increasing amount of MSW and lack of MSWM has led to the emergence of various environmental, ecological, and health hazards, which can be checked through Integrated Sustainable Solid

Waste Management (ISSWM) (Scheinberg et al., 2010). Wilson et al. (2013) suggest that the ISSWM takes into consideration the two important aspects of MSWM: (a) the governance structures i.e. the administrative set-up which comprises of public–private-partnerships, financial stability of the management systems, MSWM proactive policies and its legal framework, and (b) the physical elements including collection, recycling, treatment and disposal including the intensive processes to control the contamination produced due to mishandling of MSWM.Therefore, Scheinberg et al., (2010) and Wilson et al., (2013) proposed that analysis of current situations and practices of MSWM in the developing countries could help in understanding the challenges in attaining sustainable solutions for MSWM.

Scheinberg et al., (2010) define MSWM as analysis and classification of types of generators and types of wastes, and gradually increase the precision with which diverse MSW are directed towards appropriate and specific management subsystems. Thereby inducing modifications that have wide effects. Also highlighting that most of the developing countries, their cities still retain their informal recycling systems, i.e., material recovery which act as a potential source of livelihood for vast numbers of the urban poor. Besides, MSW is also responsible for leachate formation, landfill gases emission, and soil contamination, which directly or indirectly affect the environment, public health, and ecology (Tchobanoglous et al., 1993).

The contaminants and pollutants of MSW are widely spread all around and most of the people who are exposed to it belong to the young population of the community (Giusti, 2009). As Raj and Raj (2015) based on Census 2011 suggest that during 2001-11, the highest inhabited district of Bihar is Patna. In addition, most of the inhabitants are youth because of the fact that Bihar has India's largest concentration of population in the age cohort of below 25 years. This cohort comprises 39.30 per cent of the total population of Bihar (Kumar, 2014). The youth sub-group of the population is most active and most mobile fraction of the community, thus facing maximum exposure of MSW and subsequently are more prone to and Patna City. In 2020, two of these circles- Pataliputra and New Capital- were subdivided in two more circles, thus having a total of six circles. However, when our project was conducted there were only four circles existing, hence all analysis is presented based on those four circles. For the project we selected one or two regions from each circle such as from: (i) New Capital circle: Bailey road and Boring road regions, (ii) Patliputra circle: Patliputra region, (iii) Kankarbagh circle: Kankarbagh region and (iv) Patna City circle: Patna City region. These selected regions possess all the major sources of MSW generation like private and government offices, housing facilities, restaurants, informal market places, housing facilities, commercial areas and market places, colleges, railway station, small scale industries, shopping malls, hospitals, hotels and restaurants, schools, bus station, educational institutions, health care facilities, and riverbank of Ganga.

According to Das (1992), Patna is the land of paradoxes. Das (*ibid*) in his book the *Republic of Bihar* recognises that here wealth exists but there is no investment because of lawlessness. In Bihar, plenty also takes a back seat to the comfort of middle men and landlords. This is about the land, we ponder, which has been renowned in the past for good education, good governance, and worthy ways of life. The history of ancient India is the history of ancient Bihar. But unfortunately all these significant achievements appear to have left no living legacy for contemporary Bihar. If there are few millimetres of rain in the state capital, Patna, residents are fearful that the city will soon resemble a flooded locale as the drainage system of the city is in abysmal state. To reiterate, there is filth and stink everywhere including New Capital/Nutan Anchal region (the study area) where the relatively rich and the affluent reside. Several bureaucrats and political leaders live in this area. Many national and international non-governmental organisations have their regional office in this part of the city. It covers more than half of the total area of the city and has the highest population thus generating maximum amount of solid waste.

Present scenario of Patna

The growing economy of Patna (Gross Domestic Product (GDP) of 590.01 US$ per capita) witnessed accelerated MSW generation rate (0.037 kg/capita/day) during the year 2010-11. These statistics have been calculated on the basis of Economic Survey Report, 2011; Census, 2011; and CPCB, 2015 report data respectively. In 2011, the total quantity of MSW generated in Patna ranged from 0.08237- 0.292 million tones MSW per year (Bhanu and Kumar, 2014; CPCB, 2015). In Patna, the rural migrants who settled in the city experience various lifestyle changes. Such changes can significantly alter the consumer behavioural pattern; they prefer to purchase packaged foods and goods as daily usable. Eventually this enhances the amount of recyclables in MSW (Zurbrugg, 2003; Raj and Raj, 2015). According to these studies, MSW composition varies considerably among developing countries and their cities due to different cultures, climatic conditions, livelihood patterns, lifestyle practices, and dietary habits. In Patna also, the same scenario of MSW composition has been observed.

MSW of Patna consists nearly 49 per cent of organic waste; 12.5 per cent of total recyclables, and 38.5 per cent of others of total MSW respectively (*ibid*). In MSW composition, the category of others comprises of rubber, ash, multi laminates, appliances, e-waste, construction and demolition waste, and other inert substances (Raj and Singh, 2017). Specifically, total recyclables subsidies 12.5 per cent of total MSW, in which maximum fraction belongs to plastic (6%) and remaining goes to textile (5%), paper (4%), leather (2%), and metal (1%) (Pandey, 2014).

In terms of MSW collection system of Patna, till 2014 there was no proper door-to-door collection (Bhanu and Kumar, 2014). During 2002, a NGO called *Nidan*, had piloted the door-to-door MSW collection through involvement of MSW sanitary workers. But, due to the non-cooperative behaviour of Patna Municipal Cooperation (PMC) functionaries the MSW collection system could not last for long (NIUA, 2015). Still, on the demand of public, door-to-door collection is performed on a very small scale by *Nidan* along with some other NGOs like Clean India. Due to lack of community bins and unawareness among public, MSW is found thrown on roadsides or any other vacant landscape nearby the residential areas. Rotten MSW on the streets not only occupy the road space but also attract flies and mosquitoes to carry pathogens, for instance malaria, diarrhoea, dysentery, etc. The local authorities are unable to collect MSW on regular basis. PMC sanitary workers could only collect 65 per cent of the total MSW generated in Patna (UD and HD, 2010; Bhanu and Kumar, 2014). Such a scenario of MSW and lack of MSWM can cause traffic jams and expose people to hazardous pollutants.

The open transportation vehicles have been in practice for the collection of MSW from community bins to disposal sites identified by PMC, through tractors, regular trucks, and tricycles without any proper maintenance (BUIDCO and UD and HD, 2014; Bhanu and Kumar, 2014; Pandey, 2014; Gandhe and Kumar, 2016). During 2014, unscientific methods of disposal and treatment were widely popular, such as open burning and open dumping (BUIDCO and UD and HD, 2014; Bhanu and Kumar, 2014; Pandey, 2014). PMC manually collected MSW from 72 wards and without any scientific treatment and safe disposal it was being dumped at a dumping site of Bairiya village (Bhanu and Kumar, 2014). Local authorities after examining environmental impact of MSW in a particular area of approximately 78-80 acres designated that area for engineered landfills. It was also identified as safe site for Waste-to-Energy plant (ibid; BUIDCO and UD and HD, 2014). However, most of MSW without any treatment is being dumped on the site of landfill, also no waste to energy plant has been found active (BUIDCO and UD and HD, 2014). Such unsafe practices of MSWM have led to air, water, and land pollution. Bad odour and presence of scavenger birds contribute to serious health hazards among the people living around that area (Kumari et al., 2011; Bhanu and Kumar, 2014; Pandey, 2014). Specifically, the young population because of their frequent traveling activities have enhanced and prolonged the exposure to hazardous pollutants present in the polluted atmosphere. After this, the primary immune response to the infection has been found in the respiratory system of youth (Giusti, 2009).

Table 5: Source of MSW generation in selected regions of Patna

Circles	Region	Source of production of MSW
New Capital	Bailey Road	Concentration of private and government offices, housing facilities, restaurants, informal market places and housing facilities.
	Boring Road	Dense commercial area and market places, housing areas, colleges, railway station, hotels and restaurants.
Patliputra	Patliputra region	Small scale industries, shopping mall, concentration of commercial area, hospitals, hotels and restaurants, schools.
Kankarbagh	Kankarbagh region	Dense low and high income housing facilities, schools, market places, concentration of private hospitals, bus station.
Patna City	Patna city region	Concentration of educational institutions, health care facilities, commercial area, river bank of Ganga, dense housing facilities.

Source: Developed by authors.

For this book from each circle one or two regions has been selected. All these selected places comprised of dense gathering of people with different mindsets, hence offered the best circumstance to analyse and observe the public behaviour and awareness for MSW and MSWM.

The Scenario of Municipality Solid Wastes in Patna

This book focuses on the MSW in Patna and its significant effect on people's health. Hence it becomes imperative to explore and study about the preventive measures for scientific management of MSW for reducing the health hazards among residents of Patna.

and publication of annual reports. The Ministry of Environment, Forestry and Climate Change (MoEFCC), however prescribes different guidelines for MSWM in hilly region.

MoEFCC is the apex body for administering the nationwide execution of these MSW laws. The primary concern of MoEFCC is to implement the set of rules and programmes connecting MSW and lack of MSWM, for prevention and control of pollution and its hazardous impact on ecosystem (UD and HD, 2012). The Central Pollution Control Board (CPCB) acts as a technical wing of MoEFCC which is a countrywide environmental pollution control body, which oversees the activities of respective state pollution control boards by aiding technological support, guidance, and resolving local disagreement between different municipalities. The authorities reported that these disagreements are mainly due to paucity of technologies of MSWM or disposal grounds for MSW. They recalled that during 2011 there was some dispute of recycling of MSW at Muzaffarpur municipal body as it has this facility of recycling. But, the Muzaffarpur municipal body did not agree to extend the facility for the same, citing the overload and overwork of machines, despite efforts from Bihar State Pollution Control Board. The state governing bodies are authorised to adopt the most suitable methods for MSW collection, transportation, treatment and disposal under the guidelines of national legislation. The governing bodies are also authorised to generate funds for these activities. The decision-making of MSWM, its technical and financial support requires appropriate technical guidance and infrastructure development which comes from Bihar Urban Infrastructure Development Corporation (BUIDCO) and Urban Development and Housing Department (UD and HD).

Municipal Corporation/Urban Bodies such as PMC is mainly responsible for the door-to-door collection of MSW sweeping of streets, transportation, treatment and disposal operations, waste to energy plant, and recycling and recovery facilities. Nevertheless, municipal cooperation remains under insufficient financial limitations and therefore PMC in 2009 started inviting contracts from private sector for hiring MSWM services (BUIDCO, UD and HD, 2014). This information was also disseminated during the stakeholder's discussion regarding "Issues in Solid Waste Management" workshop held on October 11, 2014, at IIT Patna.

Now all 72 wards are working in Public-Private-Partnership (PPP) for door-to-door collection and transportation of MSW and this method was gaining some success. The authorities and functionaries pointed out that the management of MSW was problematic more due to the attitudinal problems of people and not lack of awareness. The Private Formal Division, within the administrative hierarchy of PMC, is responsible for the execution and monitoring of performance and processes of most of the door-to-door collection, their transportation to the dumping site, which may go for treatment, and disposal of MSW. This information was confirmed by other officials. The Private Informal Division MSW collectors both from the government sector and private sector usually belong to the deprived economic and social conditions (Madhav, 2010).

MSW generation and composition

Until 2011 the MSW produce in Patna was 225.67-800.00 tonne/day, which has been significantly lower than in developed countries cities (Pandey, 2014). But, reports from various government organisations suggest the raising generation rate of MSW per day. Patna produces approx. 1000-1200 tonne of MSW per day and the per capita MSW per day is 0.450-0.600 kg during 2016-17. From site visits it was evident that though the landfill in Patna exists but the condition of that landfill is deplorable. It was also noted that the landfill at Bairiya was more of a dumping ground that has no rules for regulating the waste disposal and it was necessary for the PMC to be active in imposing rules on this dumping ground. Thus, there was an urgent need to speed up the processes of MSW management.

In 2014, BUIDCO had projected the population growth of Patna by 2036 and also calculated the amount of MSW generated per day with such an exponential rise in population growth till 2036. The synchronisation of rising MSW and rapid urban population growth helps to explain that during the year 2016, 2026 and 2031 the percentage increase of MSW per day would be ten percent more than the percentage of population increase. The year 2021 and 2036 population growth percentage increase is 12.30 per cent and 11.78 per cent respectively. That is less than the percentage increase of MSW produce per day in Patna during these years, i.e., approx. 6.26 per cent and 0.01 per cent respectively.

From the workshops organised at IIT Patna during 2014 and 2015 along with field interviews, was noticed that segregation of MSW at source has not been in practice. Beside this, due to unawareness among people, the storage of MSW at source has been done in plastic buckets and plastic carry bags. Later that is thrown in low lying areas and road sides.Door-to-door collection of MSW has been initiated by PMC and UD and HD in sixteen wards of Patna during 2016 (PMC, 2013). Later during 2017 almost from 60 wards door-to-door collection of MSW has successfully been achieved via PPP approach. This door-to-door collection system under PPP has been executed on monthly charges and has been a success in the New Capital circle region of PMC.

The payment basis for door-to-door collection of MSW in wards excluded the houses below poverty line, and for the rest every house availing the services had to pay Rs 60 per month. The charges were different for commercial establishments such as small shopkeepers with shops within 10 feet of road have to pay Rs 60 per month; big shopkeepers are charged Rs 300 per month; restaurants/hotels/hostel need to pay Rs 1000 per month; five and four star hotels are charged Rs 10,000 per month; commercial establishments/government offices/banks/insurance companies/coaching institutions area to pay Rs 1000 per month; hospitals with fifty beds are to pay Rs 3000 per month; hospitals with more than fifty beds require to pay Rs 10,000 per month and other clinics and dispensaries are charged Rs 1,000 per month. Secondary collection system has been accomplished by PMC and under PPP model through selected NGOs and private companies. In secondary collection system, community bins and MSW collecting vehicles are used. These vehicles go for door-to-door collection of MSW or the communities themselves bring MSW to designated points. PMC has demarcated about 870 community bin points for secondary collection, beside this several open areas in the locality are also being used by people as unauthorised secondary collection points.

At all the designated points PMC has placed almost 550 community bins with the capacity of 1.1 m^3. But during one of the detailed interviews with the officials it was confirmed that between 2016 and 2017 approximately 320 more community bins have been placed. However, such views were contradicted by private stakeholders that these bins are placed far away from the communities and near the road sides, hence it affects the idea of secondary collection points also hampering the process of carrying out door-to-door collection and simultaneous dumping of the collected MSW into PMC designated community bins. In June 2017, PMC introduced *Bihar Municipal Act*, 2007 which required the people of Patna to ensure segregation of dry and wet MSW at the primary origination points i.e. at homes. As per the Act, wet waste are those that include the biodegradable/compostable MSW, whereas dry waste means the recyclable fraction of MSW. To advertise and sensitise the importance of segregation of waste at origin, the PMC on World Environment Day 2017, set up two colour coded dustbins at Maurya Lok Complex which is the commercial hub of Patna and also houses many official buildings. The colours represent the type of waste to be put into the dustbin-green colour dustbin for wet waste or biodegradable MSW, and blue dustbin has to be used for dry waste or recyclable MSW. PMC has been planning to place 2000 pair of colour coded community bins at the authorised destinations having a capacity of 0.12 m^3 (Nithya et al., 2013). As well as, 750 more community collection bin points are under planning to be authorised. In these points, larger capacity bins of approximately. 2-5m^3 have been made up of concrete known as RC bins will be placed soon (BUIDCO, UD and HD, 2006; Nithya et al., 2013).

The frequency of MSW removal from community bins is regular in most of the areas. Daily transportation of MSW from secondary collection points to the disposal or treatment site in Patna follows the schedule of 6:00 am to 2:00 pm excluding Sundays and holidays. But residents in certain areas of Patna disagreed with the information of PMC and mentioned that the frequency of MSW collection from homes or secondary collection points by the PMC sanitary workers were very erratic, this collection generally varied between 3-4 days in their locality. They also complained during interviews that the workers were not ready to register any grievances.

The usage of compactors which compress collected MSW at source was a heavy vehicle and thus it becomes difficult for this machine to access places that have large amount of collected MSW near community bins or informal dumping grounds in the neighbourhoods. Hence, field visits suggested that it was almost impossible for the workers to manage time schedules of collection and transfer of MSW eventually leading to accumulation of MSW in the locality.Since the waste is not segregated at source, the overall collected MSW is mostly mixed. This harmful mixed MSW, is loaded with the help of mechanical loaders and manual labours in tractors, dumper placer, and compactors. Then this collected MSW is transferred to its final destination at landfill Bairiya. It was observed during fieldwork that most of the vehicles used for transportation required serious maintenance or better replacement, specifically for tractors. It was only in the end of 2016 that new compactors and auto-tippers were introduced in the MSW transportation. But still older tractors were not replaced and were used for transportation.

It was observed and revealed in the interviews at the PMC office that there was acute shortage of proper transportation machines. According to information from PMC there were only 155 tractors and 155 auto-tippers for collection from narrow lanes. There were 20 dumper placers and 16 compactors to collect MSW from broader or main roadside community bins. In addition there were approximately 371 handcarts/tricycles for primary collection of MSW for door-to-door collection and bring it to the community bins.

The MSW collected from community bins is directly transferred to landfilling site at Bairiya. Hoornweg and Bhada-Tata (2012) in their study suggest that it is important to dispose off biodegradable

MSW within 10 hours of collection because after that the waste starts decomposing and can create serious health problems from vector borne diseases. One of the municipal officials at PMC said that it is taken care that the biodegradable wastes are not kept for more than 24 hours. The collected MSW was transferred to Bairiya every evening but at times it is difficult to follow this time frame. He also mentioned during interview that the collection of MSW was more challenging task as there were not much facilities available for it.

To overcome this challenge of excess collected MSW for transfer to dumping sites a report by BUIDCO suggests that there should be a transfer station for each circle. These transfer stations would function as proper storage for collected MSW. The same report mentions that this provision should be available for all the six circles of the PMC. However, during the interview none of the officials were able to answer satisfactorily about this provision. Rather they stated that even if there was any provision it would be difficult for PMC to acquire lands for these transfer station.

MSW treatment and disposal

The UD and HD report (2010) found that in Patna, about 65 per cent of the total MSW was being collected and the remaining 35 per cent remained unattended, strewn beside roads, also near parks, playgrounds and vacant lands. Bhanu et al., (2014) also reported in their study that in Patna there are no proper treatment and disposal method of MSWM. Hence, it had become normal to use open low-lying areas, and the outskirts of the city besides the existing dumping ground, at Bairiya. Such unscientific methods, Kumari et al., (2011), argue cause immense air and groundwater pollution. It was also evident from their study that the air quality and groundwater for a range of physiochemical parameters were beyond the permissible limit at two dumping sites in Patna where they conducted their experiments.

In Patna, the dumping ground is situated at Ilahibagh, Ramachak-Bairiya village with the land areas of approximately 74 acres. Patna has reserved it for development of WTE plant including sanitary landfill (BUIDCO, UD and HD, 2014). The landfill site at Bairiya is surrounded by six densely populated villages whose total population is estimated to be around 20,000. MSW is dumped only to Bairiya landfill besides Gardanibagh. The habitants near Bairiya landfill are facing environmental problems and chronic health issues such as respiratory tract inflammation, permanent respiratory problems as the smoke produced due to unsafe burning of MSW being dumped since 2010 consist of high amount of pollutants (Bhanu et al., 2014). The villagers filed a petition against the Bairiya landfill site in Patna High Court in November 2012. As per the Master Plan 2031, Ramchak Bairiya area has again been suggested as a sanitary landfill and WTE plant site. Nevertheless, PMC considers it as MSW mismanagement and misunderstanding of MSWM project (Bhanu et al., 2014).

Public Private Participation

According to Public-Private-Participation (PPP) for MSW treatment in Patna during 2009, UD and HD authorities under PPP agenda hired A2Z infrastructure Pvt. Ltd. of New Delhi for nine wards' door-to-door MSW collection; drainage cleaning; street sweeping mechanically, and collected MSW transportation to a designated disposal site. A2Z stated the MSW management since January 2010 and continued till July 2011, but after that the work was discontinued. The primary reason was that PMC has not been provided with the bided amount of money (i.e., approximately Rs 7.62 crores) to A2Z. In the year 2012, BUIDCO once again followed the PPP model for MSWM in Patna and Jindal ITF Urban Infrastructure Private Limited was selected, but this company refused to sign on agreement clause. PMC again floated the PPP tender agenda in 2013, but private firms showed least interest in city waste management. To attract the attention of private contractors in 2014, few features were added to the PPP agenda. That is MSW door-to-door collection and transport to the secondary destination, or PMC provided community bins without any user charges. The PMC and BUIDCO hired a Mumbai based private company named

Sunil HiTech Engineers Limited (SHEL) in 2014 for handling the MSW management of Patna. But, during the interview with PMC officials and as the PMC commissioner addressed in the workshop at IIT Patna, SHEL has failed to manage the city's MSW. According to BUIDCO in spite of various warning letters, no progress was observed in SHEIL services. Hence, work was discontinued.

But, a pilot PPP project in sixteen wards was started by PMC during 2016. According to it each house had to pay Rs 60 - Rs 70 per month for door-to-door MSW collection. The project was initiated by Nishka private firm Clean India NGO, and *Nidan* Swacchdhara Private Limited in New capital and Patliputra circle. Delhi based private firm Patheya handled the MSW at Kankarbagh and Bankipore circle. This PPP mode was able to cover 52 wards in four circles whereas tender was still open to remaining 20 wards of Patna city and Azimabad circle. But during field visits PMC sanitary workers were found working in both the circles. The PPP waste to energy project was still in progress, Patna Green Energy Private Limited was asked to develop the complex for production of 10 MW of electricity from MSW during 2016. But, their work was questioned by BSPCB. PMC official told during field interview that presently they were expecting a US-based company, AG Dauters Waste Processing Private Limited, to establish waste to energy plant in Patna.

MSWM through informal Recycling

The sanitary workers and ragpickers are the main recyclable collectors from MSW informal recycling hierarchy. Sanitary workers collect the recyclables during door-to-door collection of MSW and during dumping the MSW in community bins. These sanitary workers are also called as *safai mitras*, few of them work under PMC and majority of them belong to NGOs through PPP with PMC. Rag pickers are roaming recyclables collectors and collect the recyclables from MSW dumping grounds and community bins. The third types of recyclable collectors are *kabadiwala*, who collect the valuable recyclables from households in return of money according to its rates (per kg). The next level in the hierarchy is the stationary dealers. The MSW collected by sanitary workers, ragpickers and *kabadiwala* is sold to small dealers. The small dealers sell a bulk amount of recyclables to medium dealers and medium dealers to recycling units. However, due to the absence of recycling units in Bihar, the transporter usually transport the collected scrap to recycling units situated in other states like Gujarat. In India, poor economic conditions, ample labour and creativeness from waste resources have resulted in informal practices of MSW recycling. Also approximately 92 per cent of the people involved at the collection level of MSW recycling hierarchy are women who have pathetic economic and social situation (Gunsilius et al., 2011; Madhav, 2010).

MSW collection, transportation, treatment and final disposal are performed by formal or by the partnership of formal and informal sector. But the MSW load has been reducing completely by the informal sector through recovering of recyclables to run the scrap business. Patna generates recyclables approximately 104-117 tonne per day, which has been majorly collected by informal sector (NIUA, 2015; Pandey, 2014). The collected items include plastic, textile, paper, leather and metal undergoes recycling. Also, the recovery of recyclables decreases the load on MSW final disposal stream. Field interviews and interaction during workshops with different stakeholders resulted in facts that recycling and recovery are running at good pace but entirely via informal sector.

Public awareness and education

This section, apart from data collected from the field also correlates information from the two workshops held at IIT Patna at different times on MSW management. Mentioning these workshops are important since they focused mainly on Patna. The first workshop, the Issues in Solid Waste Management Workshop was organised on October 11, 2014 dealing specifically with management of MSW produced. The second workshop was on Effective Pedagogy for Waste Management in April 18, 2015. It dealt especially with the scenario of MSW and its management and processes to create awareness, educate and encourage active involvement of people of Patna.

The first workshop focused on paradigm shift which was required in the approaches of MSWM. This workshop provided opportunities to diverse participants (i) to develop an understanding for issues related to MSWM in Patna; and (ii) share their scientific ideas that could help in managing MSW of Patna efficiently. The discussion ranged from involving and utilizing the latest technologies and methodologies that could be used for MSWM. This workshop also highlighted the problems and possible methods upon how to include these modern control measures in Patna to reduce/manage MSW. The issue of increasing MSW was a concern then also and continues to be so in the present.

In the workshop keynote speaker Prof. Ashok Ghosh, who was then the Professor in Charge, Department of Environment and Water Management, A. N. College Patna. He emphasised on two major issues of MSWM in Patna (a) shortage of MSW management facilities, and (b) lack of awareness and communication regarding MSW management among the common public. He added that this was due to the absence of planning and management at the institutional level the PMC. Then he went on to cite that there was acute lack of data on MSW produced in the city. Prof. Ghosh also added that whatever data were collected was disorganised which made them useless or unusable.

The PMC does not and cannot control the growing menace of MSW in Patna alone said Prof. Ghosh, hence it seeks help and is guided by both governmental and NGOs. The governmental organisations include BUIDCO, UD and HD, BSPCB and SEIAA. These organisations provide monitoring as well as infrastructure help. While the non-governmental organisations such as *Nidan*, Clean India, A2Z infrastructure private limited, NSPL, SHEL, Nishka private firm, Patheya and Patna Green Energy Private Limited. Jindal ITF urban Infrastructure Private Limited, these agencies basically help in MSW management. These firms from time to time have helped the PMC to plan and execute the collection, transportation and treatment of MSW.

workshop concluded that public awareness and education can play a vital role to achieve proper MSWM. Thereby opening up a new area of probe as to how education can play a dynamic role in promoting public awareness about MSWM among people in Patna.

This workshop saw initiation of another workshop again at IIT Patna on the issue of Effective Pedagogy for Waste Management on April 18, 2015. In this study, these workshops helped to frame questions to be asked during the fieldwork and understand the shortcomings that existed in the field. The previous workshop helped reason the situation of MSW in Patna and the institutional shortcomings, culminating on to highlight the basic cause of this-lack of public awareness about MSW management. The second workshop, Effective Pedagogy for Waste Management, outlined the concerns that were required to address the issues from people's perspectives.

The field research also suggested that the basic cause of MSW mismanagement was due to attitudinal problem of the community. People were excessively dependent on the responsibility of the governmental agencies. Moreover, case studies by Ojok et al., (2014), Raj and Raj (2015 and 2018) show that public involvement plays a crucial role in MSWM. Therefore, it is important to create awareness among the community stakeholders about the importance, necessity, and their role in MSWM to reduce various environmental and health hazards. The United Nations Environment Programme (UNEP), also suggests that to curb the problems of MSW, anywhere it is important to start with children because that would make a more profound impact on the society as whole. The report also emphasises that children also influence adult behavioural patterns. Hence, the UNEP lays emphasis on creating awareness directed through children which would eventually help develop a habit of cleanliness and sanitation in coming generations (UNEP, 2011).

Therefore, the second workshop on Effective Pedagogy for Waste Management on April 18, 2015, intended to particularly involve school teachers from different educational institutions in and around Patna. A school teacher plays very significant role in shaping our behaviour through their students. The teachers have big responsibility in shaping our tomorrow. The school teachers were engaged in this workshop to understand the effective pedagogy and practices that are useful for behavioural patterns making our surroundings a better place to live. The practices that were highlighted in this workshop were directed towards minimizing MSW generation, segregation of (biodegradable and recyclables) MSW at the source, proper handling methods, i.e. placing of MSW in colour coded bins placed at secondary collection points. The workshop also discussed about how to increase public participation in managing the local sanitary workers to ascertain timely collection of MSW from their localities. This interactive workshop, therefore, tried to look beyond the normal banking concept of management of MSW, within communities and for individuals. This was achieved through usage of problem-posing generative themes asking for mutual stakes in the improvisation of communities of practices prevailing within the localities.

This workshop attracted more than 50 prestigious schools of Patna which became a part of this workshop. These schools included participants from International School, St. Karen's High School, AVN English School, Delhi Public School Patna, Don Bosco Primary School, Kendriya Vidhyala Kankarbagh, DAV Khagaul, St. Xavier's School, G D Goenka, SVM Residential School, Kamala Nehru, Veena Vidhya Niketan, Loyola High School, St. Michael's High School, St. Jude's, Litera Valley School, Patna Central School, Tribhuvan School, St. Paul's High School, St. Joseph Convent School, Radiant International School, and also teachers from Patna University. Sixty teachers from these schools who participated were actively engaged in the problem-posing themes and thus think of creative yet effortless can-be-solutions to MSWM.

During this workshop the teachers were divided into groups for these problem-posing themes keen to learn and teach their students creative yet effortless can-be-solutions to make their students responsible citizens. Each of these groups had to discuss and explain the idea they had mapped to introduce behavioural changes in their school children and society. One of the groups tried to improvise the 3-R slogan by adding another 4-R to it. The new 4-R's being Recharge, Rethink, Repair and Repeat. The new R's the group explain- Recharge- as new thinking perspective about MSWM. Rethink- as to think before creating or throwing away of the MSW. Repair- as optimise the use and reuse of the commodities treated as MSW. Repeat- as the process of the 6-R's time and again to inculcate behavioural changes in the management of MSW. The group named this 7-R's presentation as "Earth Changers" arguing that this would not only maximise the segregation but also minimise the production of MSW at source through curbing conspicuous consumption which has led to more production of MSW in Patna (Raj and Raj, 2015). These two workshops have helped this study by grooming it in the early stages of its conception. Thereby, directing the researcher to ask relevant and informed questions in the field with the stakeholders at the institutional as well as citizen's participation levels. Hence, these two workshops were mutually complementing each other to understand the process of collection, transportation and treatment of MSW in Patna.

Looking ahead

Chhat puja conveys a totally different scenario in Patna. The streets are neat and clean. Production or disposal of waste is done with utmost care. During the build up to this festival, celebrated six days after Diwali, behaviour pattern and attitude of residents, governance, and other stakeholders are seen to have totally changed. People seem to care for their locality. Devotees put emphasis on recognising the cosmos and the source of energy. This does provide a silver lining for a better Patna. We believe that change in attitude will change behaviour pattern of people here in Patna as well as any other place struggling to properly dispose off their wastes. One can have awareness raising programmes that can be supported by the community and the local governance. The awareness programmes must put emphasis on connecting people with their local community as well as with the larger environmental hazards. Increasing interest and motivation has no effect if it is not followed up by resources, support and structural improvements which make it possible, sensible, and normal for consumers to change their routines, habits and daily consumption practices.

5

Conclusion

Waste generation amidst Covid pandemic

With changes in lifestyles and consumption habits, supply chain interruptions, waste sorting and recycling logistics, falling oil prices, and reduced demand for recycled waste, the Covid-19 outbreak has caused significant challenges for waste disposal, management, and recycling, thereby impacting the circular economy around the globe (Liu et al., 2021). This waste is not only medical, infectious, and healthcare waste but also general waste such as food waste (FW) and plastic waste (PW). There have been several literature review papers on FW and PW issues published in recent years. For example, Muriana (2017) assessed the use of mathematical models in FW and loss and clarified FW's dependency on supply chain strategies. Review studies on consumer-led FW in particular have increased since private households were identified as key actors in FW generation in developed economies (Aschemann-Witzel et al., 2015). Reynolds et al. (2017) reviewed the literature on FW prevention at the consumption stage. Roodhuyzen et al. (2019) developed a framework that conceptualised the generation of consumer FW in relation to stages of the household supply chain and categorised several potential factors of consumer FW into four groups such as behavioural, personal, product, and societal factors. Schanes et al. (2018) reviewed the rising number of empirical studies on consumer FW practices and the factors that foster and impede the generation of FW at the household level. These studies represent FW to be a complex and multi-faceted issue that cannot be attributed to a single component. Because of the complexity, many literature sheds light on food-related practices, like planning and shopping, storing, cooking, eating, and managing uneaten food by adopting theories and other conceptual methods to prevent food wastage. Several FW and PW reduction targets had been set before the onset of this global crisis, including Sustainable Development Goal 12.3 which targets to reduce per capita global FW at the retail and consumer levels by half till 2030, as well as manage and control waste emissions and reduce marine pollution (Liu et al., 2021).

Several countries had issued bans on specific plastic products, optimistic in the hope of reducing the serious environmental pollution. However, the advent of the Covid-19 pandemic has aggravated the issue of FW and PW management. Single-use plastic usage is expected to snap back due to growing concerns with hygiene (such as physical distancing, gloves, masks, packaging, etc.) and increased demand for online shopping during the pandemic. Besides, household FW generation may abate along with the trends of more conscious food management during lockdowns due to fear and anxiety associated with logistic systems amidst concerns about food shortages (Sharma et al., 2020; Pappalardo et al., 2020; Jribi et al., 2020). Lockdowns did effect consumer behaviour and attitudes towards FW and PW due to changes in lifestyle habits. A study by Liu et al. (2021), based in Bangkok concludes that travel bans and diminished economic activity due to Covid-19 have led to a dramatic reduction in waste from the business sector and in the total amount of municipal waste generated. However, the results of the survey showed that both food and plastic waste generated by households increased during Covid-19. The transition from dining out to online food delivery services led to an increase in plastic bags, plastic containers, and FW. Reasons for the increase in household FW during Covid-19 varied, with respondents citing excessive amounts of food and bad taste, followed by exceeding the expiration date and rotting smell. A case study examining the impact of changing lifestyle on municipal solid waste generation in Qatar indicates direct relationship between the rising population and the high waste generation (Bello, 2018). The study found that majority of the respondents generate kitchen wastes from their households which reflects that the respondents mostly eat at home, which naturally results in kitchen waste. A good number of respondents generate paper and cardboard waste (69%), plastic waste (66%), and Nylon (54%) whereas only a few respondents generate glass waste (25%), metal waste (9%), and wood and furniture waste (4%) daily. The study gathered that household wastes are collected from the residential areas by the municipalities for free and most of the respondents do not sort their household wastes before disposal.

Pal and Bhatia (2022) have also demonstrated the increasing threat of MSW in India. They argue that SWM system is not much more efficient due to some hindrances such as waste policy, lack of the latest technique for collection, financial assistance, lack of infrastructure, and well-trained people. To achieve sustainable SWM in India, waste-to-energy facilities, recycling, and minimisation of waste generation have to be emphasised.

Towards creating a Parallel pandemic due to mis-management of wastes in Patna

Based on our studies carried out in Patna, we contend that the production of MSW has a strong association with the changing conspicuous consumption patterns with no regard for the environment. The Covid pandemic has further complicated the problem in Patna and is creating a parallel pandemic like situation. In the recent past, the spread of Covid -19 has adversely affected all spheres of our lives. This unprecedented situation has set in a new normal challenging many conventional practices. We have learnt to inculcate certain behavioural changes, such as physical distancing, wearing mask and gloves, face shields, using sanitisers, and use PPE kits. The periodical lockdowns and restrictions on mobility has increased online shopping, including medical products especially among the middle class. Also, there is panic buying including that of medicines and aided equipments. Though these behavioural changes are with a very noble intent, yet, they are not devoid of consequences that are environmentally not so viable. A point in case could is the increased consumption of medical and allied products which in turn has produced enormous amount of untreated bio-medical wastes. Our research suggests that in the first phase of the pandemic, generation of such wastes was confined mainly to medical institutions such as hospitals. The media was prompt to highlight these issues because it was evident that our municipal systems were not equipped enough to deal with this unfathomable amount of wastes. Situations in cities like Patna, where there is only one facility to treat bio-medical wastes plant at Indira Gandhiji Institute of Medical Sciences (IGIMS), is alarming. We know that there had been problems of transporting such wastes in Patna from various parts of the city even prior to the spread of Covid. When the administration was still struggling to strategise management of bio-medical wastes, the relaxed lockdown norms added more woes. Mobility of people increased and so increased vulnerability due to unattended Covid waste.

Covid appropriate behaviour is expected to be followed. But, in it there is no guidelines for how to dispose waste generated by practices in trying to protect from Covid virus. For instance, airlines have followed protocols and made sure that the crew as well as the passengers were provided with necessary gears, such as face shield, masks, PPE kits, and so on. But, in the whole plan there was no mention as to where to dispose these products after use. As a result people throw these like any other garbage in public dustbins which overflowed and hence the streets were strewn with used PPE kits, masks, and gloves. It was a shame to see the area near Patna airport dumped with these garbage items, which if not disposed safely would lead to spread of more infection. People became happy that the Covid statistics were steadily decreasing but they never realised that through mismanagement of wastes they have created a warehouse of breeding other pathogens which in the long run would adversely affect their health.

When people were almost getting back to their normal life, the second wave of Covid arrived like a tornado. It exposed the entire public health system, more so in Bihar. Lessons learnt and practices imbibed during the first wave were not enough to shield the community. The requirements and expectations of the mutated virus posed a great challenge to the administration as well as the community. As a consequence we had multiple sites of bio-medical waste generation which emerged as a big public health threat. Due to non-availability of required hospital beds and oxygen cylinders, people with mild symptoms were advised to be isolated in their own home. This was an intervention to stop spreading of the virus and avoid over-crowding at the hospitals. But, what this intervention did not anticipate was that many people who tested positive for the virus, did not disclose it in the community, mainly due to the social stigma of isolation being attached with Covid patients. The situation was worse in Patna where at multi-storeyed buildings there were several Covid patients in various apartments without the knowledge of the community so everybody who used the common facilities got exposed to the virus unknowingly.

Moreover, the wastes that were generated in households with Covid positive patients were mingled and collected with other household wastes which were not disposed as per required norms. Home delivery of food for Covid patients was a very supportive initiative offered by different catering services and restaurants in Patna. They delivered food in disposable containers to avoid reuse and stop spread of the virus. Unfortunately, even these disposable containers were dumped with normal household garbage thus creating greater risk for the community. Therefore, in the second wave the bio-medical wastes were not only generated at hospitals and their surroundings rather in every neighbourhood and housing societies of Patna. Even the kitchen waste has been mixed with bio-medical waste at the source. The onset of monsoon aggravated the situation. Water logging and stagnated pools of water is a common problem that every one in Patna has to deal with in each monsoon season. All open drains and by-lanes in Patna become sites of waste disposal, where these days along with plastic bags and wrappers, a common site noticed is floating of used masks and syringes and we have got used to these without being concerned about their repercussions.

Recent research in Maharashtra has stated that one of the main reasons for the high rate of Covid positive cases in the state can be attributed to improper management of wastes generated during the pandemic. This is an indication for us to be extra careful as in Patna we are challenged with management of MSW. A report published in *The Hindu* lists the top ten states in India with maximum amount of bio-medical waste generation in the recent past. Interestingly Bihar does not figure in the list. To most it might seem a happy scenario, but in reality it is a great concern. It clearly shows that there is under-reporting of the amount of bio-medical wastes generated in Bihar. This might be due to the fact that since most of these wastes are not separated from other wastes and do not undergo proper treatment they are not reported. Also, these wastes are strewn everywhere in the city and are not confined to specific geographical locales. As a result we need to be very cautious and take more precautions to combat the situation.

In most of the states in India generally waste management has been problematic in low-income areas, which are usually crowded, have open drains, lack proper sanitation, and also there is low awareness among people about proper waste management. But Patna presents a unique case, where field visits suggest that there is a positive correlation between lack of waste management and economic affluence of the neighbourhood. An ironic example could be of Patlipurta colony, which is supposed to be one of the most plush neighbourhood in the city, housing head offices of various international and national non-government organisations (INGOs and NGOs) working on various developmental issues. There are heaps of un-attended garbage on the roadside of this area and during the monsoon, or even if there is seasonal rainfall, this neighbourhood is almost flooded with floating garbage everywhere. During the Covid pandemic it was no exception with added amount of bio-medical wastes. It is a pity that the so-called privileged in the society are unconcerned about it as they focus on development of Bihar! They do not realise that the air they breathe does not differentiate between people of different strata and are equally toxic for one and all.

Studies have established that Corona virus affects the respiratory system and weakens it. Moreover, people with co-morbidities including respiratory issues are more vulnerable to the adverse impacts of the virus. Our research in Patna has indicated that due to improper waste management the population in Patna is very prone to both chronic and acute respiratory diseases across age groups. This created a more critical condition during the Covid pandemic. Vaccination drives were rigorously carried out to protect people from this deadly virus. Nevertheless, the wastes that have been generated and created repositories for air and water pollution cannot be protected with the Covid vaccine. To curb this the need of the hour is to educate people about proper disposal of wastes and encourage segregation of waste at source. Health education is difficult to disseminate since it is different from formal education. Of the main reasons, why health education has not been a success story in India is the fact that the medium chosen to create awareness and provide useful information had not been appropriate. For example, there had been over-reliance on printed materials and pamphlets, posters, etc. For a population with high illiteracy rate such venues to provide health education will not reach to one and all. Therefore, if appropriate medium, like advertisements in electronic and digital media, or mobile phones, that are accessible irrespective of educational status, are chosen to disseminate useful health education it will bring about desired changes. Our campaigns against fighting Covid has reiterated the importance of health education and to a large extent we were able to combat the adversities. Covid pandemic has taught us that behavioural changes can be very instrumental to avoid any epidemic. Such behavioural changes should just not be restricted to use of specific items rather it should give more emphasis on how to dispose such items after use. Otherwise, we are sitting on a time bomb. These wastes if not managed properly will create long term respiratory health hazards, especially for the young population who are most exposed to the outside world. On world plastic bag free day (July3, 2021), the Patna Municipal Corporation had adopted a good initiative to encourage people to abandon plastic bags and use handmade bags informing them about the environmental hazards of plastic bags. Similar initiatives could be launched educating people about the health hazards of improper management of MSW and encouraging them to segregate bio-medical wastes.

In this context, we would like to remind ourselves that we are getting ready to battle off various future waves of Covid pandemic, which are predicted to be more deadly, with every possible preparedness by arranging all curative measures, including availability of hospital beds, specials wards for children, enough supply of oxygen, to name a few. On the preventive front the vaccination drive has received new momentum and the numbers of vaccinated individuals are on the rise, even trials of vaccination for children are proceeding at a good pace. It would be myopic in our vision if we do not consider the role of health education to bring about health promotion that leads to sustainable good health.

It is important to set short term goals to overcome the looming pandemic. Similarly, it is equally important, if not more, to ensure that the conditions we generate in coping with the situation should not result in creating a parallel pandemic. People need to be made aware that the onus is on every individual to tackle the problem of waste disposal and waste management since all of us are responsible for waste generation. Though it is the responsibility of the municipality to collect the wastes, but at the household level we should segregate waste and mark them. If we are not willing to make the required behavioural changes in our attitude, then we might create a parallel pandemic through improper management of increasing wastes. This pandemic would be more long lasting and lethal than the Covid as it will have serious latent health effects- every day through air and water pollution it will find way to the human immune system and make our respiratory system hollow from within like a termite. The vaccines would protect us from the different variants of Corona virus, but lack of waste management will expose us to an ongoing pandemic which we consider to be part of our every day life. As soon as we unmask, these will strike us hard on the face. The improper management of waste is the most important public health challenge that we have to acknowledge, especially at a time when we are generating huge amount of bio-medical wastes. If we are reluctant to realise the seriousness about the problem of waste management, and focus only on dealing with the current pandemic at hand we would win the battle but lose the war.

The Covid pandemic requires renewed efforts to comprehend discard. While we kept battling the pandemic, we kept creating so much waste. Otherwise also, the amount of waste created is alarming. Discard studies should also look at other cases in India such as air pollution or sound pollution. Similarly, other cities can also be comprehensively studied. In fact, if we were to conduct this research now, we would draw from the work of scholars like Brouno Latour and make distinct his matter of fact and matter of concern. We would also work along the lines of waste to resource creation. In fact, one of the author, through his involvement with the *Unnat Bharat Abhiyan*, attempted for waste to resource creation in rural Patna. Role of scheduled caste in waste collection and recycling is very pertinent issue to be explored further for discard studies in India. As we conclude, we would like to point that, it is carelessness about the community which is one of the main reason for unwanted waste creation and lack of waste management. Hopefully, this book will help take steps forward for better politico-economic and social practices.

Postscript

What people do not find useful is discard. The discussion in this book is on products. The productions of these have increased in the age of rampant capitalism. More industries, more production, more consumption, and more waste. Solid waste is more visible. Solid waste management seems urgent. Integrated solid waste management will be useful. Patna is just an example. Some place is better. Some others may be worse. Historical legacy and contemporary state formation has influenced governance patterns. The governance in urban bodies like that of Patna may need more attention. Nevertheless, the problem is deep seated and pervasive.

Products that are discard are obvious. However, the processes in which these products are thought as useful while some at the stage to be discard needs comprehension. Also, what is discard of some people may be useful for another. There has been a section in our society who have made their living from the discard of common populace. Did you know about ScrapUncle? They have made recycling easy in Delhi these days. This start-up has caught attention of many as we think through our discard. They have added value to what is discard for many of us. It is a start-up and, therefore, we either know or will find out.

In Bihar, for instance, we do not have business venture dealing with discard. Whatever is collected, starting from door-to-door collection, is processed and sent to provinces like Gujarat for recycling. These door-to-door collections in rural and semi-rural places are still common in Bihar. Women-folk wait and make their small bit from domestic discard. Sometime, they get some useful kitchen utensil in exchange for their discard. Out-dated newspapers, old batteries, broken items, most of it, except electronic (e) wastes. We have found that people here hold on to their e-wastes. It is assumed that their value is still there in these e-products. Some told us that e-products were very expensive and you never know they may yet have utility left in them.

Relation with discard is presumed to be over. If not, they would be kept in possession. The relation of people with product can be extended to understand relationship of people with people. How people relate with those who (or, what) has less usefulness (or, utility) speaks volumes about their nature and conduct. It may be lower caste or class, children, or old age people. Sometimes, it is interesting to see where we have come as a community. Our traditions have plenty of examples that clearly suggests that we lived in consonance with nature. Nothing was discard. Everything had utility. People as well as products. All practices have been such that made us respect people as well as what people used (products). Now we have plenty of products and no care.

We feel modern in criticizing our traditions. Even those traditional practices which made us live in rhythm with Mother Nature appreciating our people and our products. Earlier, the community of practice meant the cosmos to its members. We have opened up and the whole globe is attested to be our home. While we proudly claim to be living in the global village, we do not know our neighbours. We do not bother to know also. Neither are we concerned about our neighbourhood. We dispose-off, what we do not need, at will- without care or concern. Our practices have started to bite us. We need to change. We need to respect even our discard. Step one- let us comprehend our discard better.

Bibliography

Abdou, H.A., Tsafack, M.D.D., Ntim, C.G. and Baker, R.D. (2016). Predicting creditworthiness in retail banking with limited scoring, Knowledge-Based Systems, 103, 89-103.

Agarwal, A., Singhmar, A., Kulshrestha, M., Mittal, A. K., (2005). Municipal solid waste recycling and associated markets in Delhi, India. Resources, Conservation and Recycling 44 , 73-90.

Ahmed, S A, Ali, S M (2006). People as partners: Facilitating people's participation in public-private partnerships for solid waste management. Habitat International 30, 781-796.

AHS, 2011. Annual health survey Bihar, fact sheet New Delhi 2010-11. Vital statistics division, office of the registrar general and census commissioner, India.

AHS, 2012. Annual health survey Bihar, fact sheet New Delhi 2011-12. Vital statistics division, office of the registrar general and census commissioner, India.

AHS, 2013. Annual health survey Bihar, fact sheet New Delhi 2012-13. Vital statistics division, office of the registrar general and census commissioner, India.

Al-Khatib, I A, Kontogianni, S, Nabaa, H A, Alshami, N, Al-Sari, M I (2015). Public perception of hazardousness caused by current trends of municipal solid waste management. Waste Management 36, 323-330.

Alagoz, A Z, Kocasoy, G (2008). Improvement and modification of the routing system for the health-care waste collection and transportation in Istanbul. Waste Management, Volume 28, Issue 8, 1461-1471.

Alam, P. and Ahmade, K. (2013). Impact of solid waste on health and the environment, International Journal of Sustainable Development, 2, 165-168.

Allesch, A, Brunner, P H (2014). Assessment method for solid waste management: A literature review. Waste Management and Resources Vol. 32, No. 6, 461-473.

An. H., Englehardtm J., Fleming, L. and Bean, J. (1999). Occupational health and safety amongst municipal solid waste workers in Florida, Waste Management Resources, 17, 369-377.

Anghinolfi, D, Paolucci, M, Robba, M, Taramasso, A C (2013). A dynamic optimisation model for solid waste recycling. Waste Management, Volume 33, Issue 2, 287-296.

Aschemann-Witsel, J.; de Hooge, I.; Amani, P.; Bech-Larsen, T.; Oostindjer, M (2015). Consumer-related food waste: Causes and potential for action. Sustainability, 7, 6457-6477.

Attri, S D, Tyagi, A (2010). Climate Profile of India, pp.2, Met Monograph No. Environment Meteorology- 01/2010, New Delhi, India: Environment Monitoring and Research Centre, India Meteorological Department, Ministry of Earth Sciences, Government of India.

Bajpai, P.K., Priya, K. and Malik, M. (2012). Selection of appropriate growth model for prediction of sugarcane area, production and productivity of India, Sugar Technology, 14, 188-191.

Bandopadhyaya, A. Bahuroopi Gandhi; Chapter 6, Scavenger. G. R. Bhatkal, Popular Prakashan, Bombay, India 1964.

Beck, Ulrich. (2009). World at Risk. Malden, MA: Polity Press.

Begum, R.A., Siwar, C., Pereira, J.J. and Jaafar, A.H. (2009). Attitude and behavioral factors in waste management in the construction industry of Malaysia, Resources, Conservation and Recycling, 53, 321-328.

Bhanu, A K, Kumar, R (2014) Strategy for Municipal Solid Waste Management: A Case Study of Patna. International Journal of Chemical, Environmental and Biological Sciences (IJCEBS) Volume 2, Issue 4, 223-227.

Blieme, F. (1973). Theil's forecast accuracy coefficient: a clarification, Journal of Marketing Research, X, 444-446.

Borthakur, A., and Govind, M. (2017). Emerging trends in consumers' E-waste disposal behaviour and awareness: A worldwide overview with special focus on India. Resources, Conservation and Recycling, 117, 102-113.

Borthakur, A., and Govind, M. (2018). Public understandings of E-waste and its disposal in urban India: from a review towards a conceptual framework. Journal of Cleaner Production, 172, 1053-1066.

Brunner, P H, Rechberger, H (2015). Waste to energy - key element for sustainable waste management. Waste Management 37, 3-12.

Buendia, M P (1998). The Waste Society: Some Elements for A Social Theory Of Waste In Modern Societies, conference paper.

BUIDC, UD and HD (Bihar Urban Infrastructure Development Corporation, Urban Development and Housing Department) Government of Bihar (2014). Development of Integrated MSW to Energy (Electricity) Processing Facility and Sanitary Landfill in Patna, Bihar on DBFOT Basis (24 March, 2014): http://urban.bih.nic.in/ (accessed January 3, 2015).

Bünger, J., Schappler-Scheele, B., Hilgers, R. and Hallier, E. (2007). A 5-year follow-up study on respiratory disorders and lung function in workers exposed to organic dust from composting plant, International Archives of Occupational and Environmental Health, 80, 306-312.

Census India, Ministry of Home Affairs, Government of India (2011) Delhi Population Census data 2011: http://www.census2011.co.in/census/state/delhi.html (accessed February 2, 2015).

Census India, Ministry of Home Affairs, Government of India (2011) Patna District: Census 2011 data: http://www.census2011.co.in/census/district/82-patna.html (accessed February 2, 2015).

Chattopadhyay, S, Dutta, A, Ray, S (2009). Municipal solid waste management in Kolkata, India – A review. Waste Management 29: 1449-1458.

Chen, X, Geng, Y, Fujita, T (2010). An overview of municipal solid waste management in China. Waste Management 30, 716-724.

Cordier, S., Chevrier, C., Robert-Gnansia, E., Lorente, C., Brula, P. and Hours, M. (2004). Risk of congenital anomalies in the vicinity of municipal solid waste incinerators, Occupational and Environmental Medicine, 61, 8-1 5.

CPCB and MoEF (2015). Status report on compliance by CPCB with municipal solid waste (management and handling) rules, 2000 New Delhi, (http://www.cpcb.nic.in/divisionofheadoffice/pcp/ msw_report.pdf. (accessed February 10, /2015)).

CW (The Collected Works of Mahatma Gandhi: August 01, 1947 – November 10, 1947). The Publications Division Ministry of Information and Broadcast Government of India, Navajivan Trust, Ahmedabad, volume 89. https://www.gandhiheritageportal.org/cwmg_volume_thumbview/MQ==#page/1/mode/2up, 1983 (Accessed 07 July 2018).

CW (The Collected Works of Mahatma Gandhi: August 1919 – July 1920). The Publications Division Ministry of Information and Broadcast Government of India, Navajivan Trust, Ahmedabad, volume 16. https://www.gandhiheritageportal.org/cwmg_volume_thumbview/MQ==#page/1/mode/2up, 1965 (Accessed 04 July 2018).

Diaz, L.F., Savage, G.M. and Eggerth, L.L. (2005). Solid Waste Management: Principles of Municipal Solid Waste Management, UNEP (United Nations Environment Programmes). 1,1.

Dong, J, Chi, Y, Zou, D, Fu, C, Huang, Q, Ni, M (2014). Comparison of municipal solid waste treatment technologies from a lifecycle perspective in China. Waste Management and Resources, Vol. 32, No.1: 13-23.

Douglas, M. 2002 [1966]. Purity and danger. London: Routledge.

Douwes, J. Thorne, P. Pearce, N. and Heederik, D. (2003). Bioaerosol health effects and exposure assessment: progress and perspectives, Annals of Work Exposures and Health, 47, 3, 187-200.

Drackner, M (2005). What is waste? To whom? – An anthropological perspective on garbage. Waste Management Research, 23, 175-81.

Dyson, B, Chang, N (2005). Forecasting municipal solid waste generation in a fast-growing urban region with system dynamics modelling. Waste Management 25, 669-679.

Economic Survey Report (2011). Economic Survey 2010-11. Patna: Finance Department of Bihar, Government of Bihar, Government of India.

Economic Survey Report (2013). Estimation of state domestic product 2012-13. New Delhi: Finance Department of Delhi, Government of Delhi, Government of India.

Elliott, P. Briggs, D. Morris, S. Hoogh, C. Hurt, C. and Jensen, T.K. (2001). Risk of adverse birth outcomes in populations living near landfill sites, BMJ, 323, 363-368. DOI: 10.1136/bmj.323.7309.363.

Erses Yay, A.S. (2015). Application of life cycle assessment (LCA) for municipal solid waste management: a case study of Sakarya, Journal of Cleaner Production, 94, 284-293. DOI: 10.1016/j.

ESR, (2011). Economic Survey Report 2010-11 Patna.

Fagan (2003). Sociological Reflections on Governing Waste. Irish Journal of Sociology 12(1). 67-84.

Floret, N. Mauny, F. Challier, B. Arveux, P. Cahn, J.Y. and Viel, J.F. Guerrero, L A, Maas, G, Hogland, W. (2013). Review Solid waste management challenges for cities in developing countries. Waste Management 33, 220-232.

Gutschmidt, K. and Vickers, C. (2010). WHO human health risk assessment toolkit: chemical hazards, IPCS harmonisation project document, Geneva, WHO Press.

H. Bello (2018). Impact of Changing Lifestyle on Municipal Solid Waste Generation in Residential Areas: Case Study of Qatar, Int. J. Waste Resource, 8(2).

Hajian-Tilaki, K. (2013). Receiver Operating Characteristic (ROC) curve analysis for medical diagnostic test evaluation, Caspian Journal of Internal Medicine, 4, 627-635.

Halla, F, Majani, B (1999). Innovative Ways for Solid Waste Management in Dar-Es-Salaam: Toward Stakeholder Partnerships. Habitat International, Vol. 23, No. 3, 351-361.

Hamer, G. (2003). Solid waste treatment and disposal: effects on public health and environmental safety, Biotechnology Advances, 22, 71-79.

Handa, K, Paul, A, Jain, P (2013). Status of composting in India with emphasis on Delhi. International Journal for Research in Applied Science and engineering technology, Vol. 1, No. 4, 60-64.

Hawkins, G. 2006. The ethics of waste. Lanham, Md.: Rowman and Littlefield.

Hazra, T, Goel, S (2009). Solid waste management in Kolkata, India: Practices and challenges. Waste Management 29, 470-478.

Hooda, R. P. (2002). Introduction to Statistics. New Delhi: Macmillan India Ltd.

Hoornweg, D, Bhada-Tata, P (2012). What a Waste; A Global Review of Solid waste Management. Washington, DC USA, Urban Development and Local Government Unit World Bank.

Hosmer, D.W., Hosmer, T., Le Cessie, S. and Lemeshow, S. (1997). A comparison of goodness-of-fit tests for the logistic regression, Statistics in Medicine, 16, 965-980.

HPSFG (Hog Producers Sustainable Farming Group), Agassiz (Pacific Agricultural Research Centre), Agriculture and Agri-Food Canada, Resource Management Branch, BCMAF (1996). Composting Methods, Composting Factsheet No. 382, 500-5, Abbotsford BC, Canada, British Columbia, Ministry of Agriculture, Food and Fisheries.

Jha, A K, Singh, S K, Singh, G P, Gupta, P K (2011). Sustainable municipal solid waste management in low income group of cities: a review. Tropical Ecology, Vol. 52, No. 1, 123-131.

Johnstone, N, Labonne, J (2004). Generation of Household Solid Waste in OECD Countries: An Empirical Analysis Using Macroeconomic Data. Land Economics, Vol. 80, No. 4, 529-538.

Joseph, K (2006). Stakeholder participation for sustainable waste management. Habitat International, 30, 863-871.

Kalyani, K A, Pandey, K K (2014). Waste to energy status in India: A short review. Renewable and Sustainable Energy Reviews, 31, 113-120.

Kaushal, R K, Varghese, G K, Chabukdhara, M (2012). Municipal Solid Waste Management in India- Current State and Future Challenges: A Review. International Journal of Engineering Science and Technology (IJEST), Vol. 4 No. 4, 1473-1489.

Koné, W.M. Vargas, M. and Keiser, J. (2012). Anthelmintic activity of medicinal plants used in Côte d'Ivoire for treating parasitic diseases, Parasitology Research, 110, 2351-2362. DOI: 10.1007/s00436-011-2771-z.

Koroneos, C.J. and Nanaki, E.A. (2012). Integrated solid waste management and energy production -a life cycle assessment approach: the case study of the city of Thessaloniki, Journal of Cleaner Production, 27, 141-150.

Kumar, S, Bhattacharyya, J K, Vaidya, A N, Chakrabarti, T, Devotta, S, Akolkar, A B (2009). Assessment of the status of municipal solid waste management in metro cities, state capitals, class I cities, and class II towns in India: An insight. Waste Management, 29, 883-895.

Kumar, R. and Indrayan, A. (2011). Receiver Operating Characteristic (ROC) curve for medical researchers, Indian Pediatrics, 48, 277-287.

Kumari, K, Ranjan, N, Sinha, R C (2011). Solid waste management in Patna - analyses of ambient air and ground water pollution. Int. J. of Environmental Technology and Management, Vol.14, No.1/2/3/4: 310 - 325.

Laitinen, S. and Rantio, T. (2016). Exposure to dangerous substances in the waste management sector, (https://oshwiki.eu/wiki/Exposure_ to_dangerous_substances_in_the_waste_management_sector (7.09.2016)).

Leach, E. 1989 [1964]. Anthropological aspects of language: animal categories and verbal abuse. Anthrozoos 2(3), 151-65.

Liu, C.; Bunditsakulchai, P.; Zhuo, Q (2021). Impact of Covid-19 on Food and Plastic Waste Generated by Consumers in Bangkok, Sustainability, 13 (8988), 1-21.

Maclaren, V.W. and Yu, C.C. (1997). Solid waste recycling behavior of industrial-commercial-institutional establishments, Growth and Change, 28, 93-109. DOI: 10.1111/1468-2257.00051.

Mandal, P, Chaturvedi, M K, Bassin, J K, Vaidya A N, Gupta R K (2014). Qualitative assessment of municipal solid waste compost by indexing method. International Journal of Recycling of Organic Waste in Agriculture, 3, 133-139.

Maridakis, S.G. Wheelwright, S.C. and Hyndman, R.J. (Eds.), (1998). Forecasting: Methods and Application, 3rd ed., John Wiley and Sons, New York 1998.

MCD (Municipal Corporation of Delhi) (2015). Solid Waste Transportation Management System: http:// mcdonline.gov.in/tri/edmc_mcdportal/dems/ (accessed June 16, 2015).

Medina, M (2010). Solid Wastes, Poverty and the Environment in Developing Country Cities Challenges and Opportunities. Econstor: United Nations University- World Institute for Development Economics Research (UNU-WIDER) No. 2010, 23, 1-15.

Meeker, J.D. Sathyanarayana, S. and Swan, S.H. (2009). Pathalates and other additive in plastic: human exposure and associated health outcome, Philosophical Transactions of the Royal Society B, 364, 2097-2113.

Melnyk, A., Kuklińska, K., Wolska, L. and Namieśnik, J. (2014). Chemical pollution and toxicity of water samples from stream receiving leachate from controlled municipal solid waste (MSW) landfill, Environmental Research, 135, 253-261. DOI: 10.1016/j.envres.2014.09.010.

Mendenhal, W. and Sincich, T. (2012). A Second Course in Statistics: Regression Analysis, 7th ed., Pearson Education, Inc., Boston, 494.

MoEF, (2016). Solid waste management rule, 2016, (http://www.moef.gov.in/sites/default/files/SWM%202016.pdf(20.07.2016).

MoEF (Ministry of Environmental and Forestry) Government of India (2000).

Municipal Solid Wastes (Management and Handling) Rules, 2000 New Delhi: http://www.moef.nic.in/legis/hsm/mswmhr.html (accessed July 23, 2015).

Moeller, D.W. (2005). Environmental Health, London: Harvard

Mondéjar-Jiménez, J.A., Ferrari, G., Secondi, L. and Principato, L. (2016). "From the table to waste: an exploratory study on behaviour towards food waste of Spanish and Italian youths", Journal of Cleaner Production, Vol. 138, 8-18.

Muriana, C. (2017). A focus on the state of the art of food waste/ losses issue and suggestions for future researches. Waste Manag, 68, 557-570.

Nag, A, Vizayakumar, K. (2005). Environmental Education and Solid Waste Management, 16. Delhi, India: New Age International.

O'Brien, M. (2008). A crisis of waste. London: Routledge.

O'Hare (2019). Waste. Economics Politics. Cambridge Encyclopaedia of Anthropology.

Pandey, M.K. (2014). Solid waste management in Patna, (http:// www.nswai.com/DataBank/Bihar_pdf/swm%20patna%201. pdf (20.08.2016)).

Pandyaswargo, A H, Onoda, H, Nagata, K (2012). Energy recovery potential and life cycle impact assessment of municipal solid waste management technologies in Asian countries using ELP model. International Journal of Energy and Environmental Engineering, 28, 3, 1-11.

Pappalardo, G.; Cerroni, S.; Nayga, R.M.; Yang, W (2020). Impact of Covid-19 on Household Food Waste: The Case of Italy. Front. Nutr, 7, 58509.

Parfitt, J., Barthel, M. and McNaughton, S. (2010). Food waste within food supply chains: quantification and potential for change to 2050, Philosophical Transactions of the Royal Society Biological Sciences, 365 (1554), 3065-3081.

Pivnenko, K., Olsson, M.E., Götze, R., Eriksson, E. and Astrup, T.F. (2016). Quantification of chemical contaminants in the paper and board fractions of municipal solid waste, Waste Management, 51, 43-54. DOI: 10.1016/j.wasman.2016.03.008.

Quested, T.E., Marsh, E., Stunell, D. and Parry, A.D. (2013). Spaghetti soup: the complex world of food waste behaviours, Resources Conservation and Recycling, 79, 43-51.

Raghu and Rodrigues (2021). A Concept of Solid Waste Management Behaviour in India – A Solution towards Environmental Sustainability. Environmental Management 22(183), 155-162.

Raj, A. and Raj, P. (2018). The global Paradox: Waste Production in Patna. In Globalisation Environment and Social Justice: Perspectives, Issue and Concerns (ed.) Manish Verma, Routedge, 163-182.

Raj, P. and Raj, A. (2015). An analysis of waste production in Patna. ISA e-symposium Sociology, 1-13.

Raj, P. and Singh, A. (2017). A Review of municipal solid waste management in developing countries, International Journal of Environment and Development, 14, 2, 234-256.

Ray, M.R., Mukherjee, G., Roychowdhury, S. and Lahiri, T. (2004). Respiratory and general health impairments of ragpickers in India: a study in Delhi, International Archives of Occupational and Environmental Health, 77, 595-598.

Reusswig, F., Lotze-Campen, H., and Gerlinger, K. (2003). Changing Global Lifestyle and Consumption Patterns: The Case of Energy and Food.

Reynolds, C.; Goucher, L.; Quested, T.; Bromley, S.; Gillick, S.; Wells, V.K.; Evans, D.; Koh, L.; Kanyama, A.C.; Katzeff, C.; et al (2019). Review: Consumption-stage food waste reduction interventions—What works and how to design better interventions. Food Policy, 83, 7-27.

Roby, E (2016). Sociological Approaches to Waste as a Social Problem: Environmental Burden, Race, Class, and Place, Conference paper, University of Buffalo.

Romieu, I., Samet, J., Smith, K.R. and Bruce, N. (2002). Outdoor air pollution and acute respiratory infections among children in developing countries, Journal of Occupational and Environmental Medicine, 44, 640-649.

Roodhuyzen, D.M.A.; Luning, P.A.; Fogliano, V.; Steenbekkers, L.P.A (2017). Putting together the puzzle of consumer food waste: Towards an integral perspective. Trends Food Sci. Technology, 68, 37-50.

Rushton, L. (2003). Health hazards and waste management, British Medical Bulletin, 68, 183-197.

Saito, N, Pathak, D R (2013). Solid Waste Management in Nepal Current Status and Policy Recommendations. Philippines: Asian Development Bank (ADB).

Sarkar, S.K., Habshah, M. and Rana, S. (2011). Detection of outliers and influential observations in binary logistic regression: an empirical study, Journal of Applied Sciences, 11, 26-35. DOI: 10.3923/jas.2011.26.35.

Sastry, R. V. Under the auspices of the servant of untouchables society: Section: An overdue civic reform. Harijan: Poona, India, Vol. 1, No. 1, 1933.

Savelli, E., Murmura, F., Liberatore, L., Casolani, N. and Bravi, L. (2019). "Consumer attitude and behaviour towards food quality among the young ones: empirical evidences from a survey", Total Quality Management and Business Excellence, 30 (1), 169-183.

Schanes, K.; Dobernig, K.; Gözet, B (2018). Food waste matters—A systematic review of household food waste practices and their policy implications. J. Clean. Prod., 182, 978-991.

Schwartz, J. (1993). Particulate air pollution and chronic respiratory disease, Environmental Research, 62, 7-13. DOI: 10.1006/enrs.1993.1083.

Seaton, A., Godden, D., MacNee, W. and Donaldson, K. (1995). Particulate air pollution and acute health effects, Lancet, 345, 176-178. DOI: 10.1016/S0140-6736(95)90173-6.

Sharholy, M, Ahmad, K, Mahmood, G, Trivedi, R C (2008). Municipal solid waste management in Indian cities - A review. Waste Management, 28, 459-467.

Sharma, H.B.; Vanapalli, K.R.; Cheela, V.S.; Ranjan, V.P.; Jaglan, A.K.; Dubey, B.; Goel, S.; Bhattacharya, J (2020). Challenges, opportunities, and innovations for effective solid waste management during and post Covid-19 pandemic. Resour. Conserv. Recycl, 162, 105052

Shekdar, A V (2009). Sustainable solid waste management: An integrated approach for Asian countries. Waste Management 29, 1438-1448.

Singh, A, Mukhopadhyay, D, Sarkar, J P, Dutta, S (2012). Biodegradation of Vegetable Solid Market Waste In presence of Plastic. Proceedings of International Conference on Environmentally Sustainable Urban Ecosystems (ENSURE 2012) Department of Civil Engineering, Indian Institute of Technology Guwahati, 24-26 February, 183-188, Guwahati: Assam, India.

Singh, A, Mukhopadhyay, D, Sarkar, J P, Dutta, S (2014). "Studies on Effect of Plastic on Biodegradation of Vegetable Solid Market Waste Through Detailed Analysis of Leachate." Journal of Solid Waste Technology and Management Volume, 40, No. 3, 266-284.

Srinivasan, K (2006). Public, Private and Voluntary Agencies in Solid Waste Management A Study in Chennai City. Economic and Political Weekly, 2259-2267.

Srivastava, V, Ismail, S A, Singh, P, Singh, R P (2014). Urban solid waste management in the developing world with emphasis on India: challenges and opportunities. Reviews in Environmental Science and Biotechnology: Epub ahead of print 8 October 2014, doi 10.1007/s11157-014-9352-4.

Stern, D I (2004). The Rise and Fall of the Environmental Kuznets Curve. World Development, Vol. 32, No. 8, 1419-1439.

Strasser, S. (1999). Waste and want. New York: Metropolitan Book.

Taiwo, A M (2011). Composting as a sustainable waste management technique in developing countries. Journal of Environmental Science and Technology 4, No. 2, 93-102.

Talyan, V, Dahiya, R P, Sreekrishnan, T R (2008). State of Municipal Solid Waste Management in Delhi, the Capital of India. Waste Management, 28, 1276-1287.

Tchobanoglous, G., Theisen, H. and Vigil, S.A. (2014). Integrated Solid Waste Management: Engineering Principles and Management Issues, Mcgraw-Hill education (Indian) Pvt. Ltd., New Delhi.

Thompson, M. (2017). Rubbish theory: the creation and destruction of value. London: Pluto Press.

Thukral, R. K., and S. Rahman (2017). Bihar Distric Factbook Patna Factbook: Key Socio-economic Data of Patna District, Bihar. 1st Edition, New Delhi: Datanet India Pvt. Ltd.

Tian, H, Gao J, Hao, J, Lu, L, Zhu, C, Qiu, P (2013). "Atmospheric pollution problems and control proposals associated with solid waste management in China: A review." Journal of Hazardous Materials 252-253, 142-154.

Troschinetz, A L, Mihelcic, J R (2009). Sustainable recycling of municipal solid waste in developing countries. Waste Management 29, 915-923.

UD and HD (2014). Master plan for Patna – 2031, (https://web. archive. org/web/20160609180331/http://urban.bih.nic.in/PMP/ Patna- MP-Report-18-11-2014.pdf (13.09.2016)).

Uiterkamp, BJS, Azadi, H., Ho, P., (2011). Sustainable recycling model: A comparative analysis between India and Tanzania. Resouces, Conservation and recycling, 55, 344-355.University Press.

USEPA (US Environmental Protection Agency) (2012). Municipal Solid Waste: http://www.epa.gov/ epawaste/nonhaz/municipal/ (accessed March 10, 2015).

Van de Klundert, A, Anschütz, J, Scheinberg, A (2001). Integrated Sustainable Waste Management - the Concept Tools for Decision-makers Experiences from the Urban Waste Expertise Programme (1995- 2001). Gouda (Netherlands): WASTE.

Vij, D. (2012). Urbanisation and solid waste management in India: Present practices and future challenges. Procedia - Social and Behavioral Sciences, 37, 437-447.

Vilavert, L. Figueras, M.J. Schuhmacher, M. Nadal, M. and Domingo, J.L. (2014). Formaldehyde: a chemical of concern in the vicinity of MBT plants of municipal solid waste, Environ. Res., 133, 27-35. DOI: 10.1016/j.envres.2014.04.041.

WHO (2017). World Health Organisation. Chronic respiratory diseases, (http://www.who.int/respiratory/about_topic/en/ (2.07.2017)). Worrell, W.A. and Vesilind, P.A. (2012). Solid Waste Engineering, 2nd ed., Cengage Learning, Stamford, USA.

Wilson, D C (2007). Development drivers for waste management. ISWA, Waste Management and Research; 25, 198-207.

Wilson, D C, Velis, C A, Rodic, L (2013). Integrated sustainable waste management in developing countries. Proceedings of the Institution of Civil Engineers, Waste and Resource Management, volume 166, Issue WR2, May 2013, 58-62.

World Bank Group: IBRD, IDA et al. (2010,2011& 2012). Economy and Growth; GDP per capita (current US$): http://data.worldbank.org/about/country-and-lending-groups (accessed January 10, 2015).

World Bank Group: IBRD, IDA et al. (2013). Country and Lending Groups: http://data.worldbank.org/ indicator/NY.GDP.PCAP.CD (accessed March 10, 2015).

Worrell, W A, Vesilind, P A (2012). Solid Waste Engineering second Edition, 64, Stamford, USA: Cengage Learning.

Zurbrugg, C (2003). Solid Waste Management in Developing Countries. Duebendorf: Scientific Committee on Problems of the Environment (SCOPE). Urban Solid Waste Management Review Session, Durban: South Africa.

Zurbrügg, C, Gfrerer, M, Ashadi, H, Brenner, W, Küper, D (2012). Determinants of sustainability in solid waste management – The Gianyar Waste Recovery Project in Indonesia. Waste Management 32, 2126-2133.

Index